Best Easy Day Hikes Austin

Keith Stelter

FALCONGUIDES

GUILFORD, CONNECTICUT
HELENA, MONTANA
AN IMPRINT OF GLOBE PEQUOT PRESS

FALCONGUIDES®

Copyright © 2009 by Morris Book Publishing, LLC

TOPO! Explorer software and SuperQuad source maps courtesy of
National Geographic Maps. For information about TOPO! Explorer,
TOPO!, and Nat Geo Maps products, go to www.topo.com or www
.natgeomaps.com.

Maps: DesignMaps Inc. © Morris Book Publishing, LLC

Library of Congress Cataloging-in-Publication Data
Stelter, Keith.
  Best easy day hikes, Austin / Keith Stelter.
      p. cm. — (Best easy day hikes series)
  ISBN 978-0-7627-5291-1
  1. Hiking—Texas—Austin—Guidebooks. 2.   Austin (Tex.)—Guide-
books. I. Title.
  GV199.42.T492A876 2009
  917.64'2520464—dc22
                                              2009022530
Printed in the United States of America
10 9 8 7 6 5 4 3 2 1

Contents

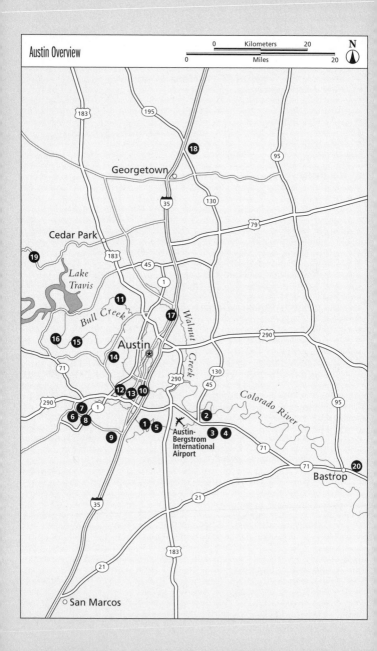

Acknowledgments

Many people helped make this book possible, and a few went beyond the call of duty. Thanks to Mark, Scott, and Kay Stelter for their encouragement, ideas, and proofreading. Karen Vasquez and Rick and Samantha Finch went hiking with me.

Thanks also to Chris Holmes, Texas Parks & Wildlife Department (TPWD) regional interpretive specialist, State Parks Region V, for working with me on new trails and the development of Texas Parks & Wildlife trail maps. Bill Beach, TPWD assistant office manager for Guadalupe River State Park, provided me with all kinds of information. Lynn Kuenstler, peace officer at Enchanted Rock State Natural Area, hiked with me and explained vernal pools.

There were many other folks at TPWD who were very helpful. At McKinney Roughs Nature Park, part of the Lower Colorado River Authority (LCRA) park system, site manager Mike McCracken and administrative associate Karen Gardner are due thanks for their assistance. Thanks to Susan Blackledge for help on the Berry Springs Park information. Allison Hardy, GIS technician with the City of Austin Parks and Recreation Department, and Dianne Hart, GIS specialist for San Antonio Natural Areas, helped with making trail maps.

There were dozens of other people who helped with information about history, geology, flora and fauna, and hikes they considered the best. I appreciate their work and thank all of them.

Introduction

The purpose of this book is to offer more than the typical hiking guide, in which most trail descriptions are generally point-to-point guides, getting you from the trailhead to the trail's end. This book provides details about flora, fauna, history, and geology to appeal to a broad spectrum of hikers, including families with young children. I spent nine months researching, talking with rangers and other folks, hiking and sometimes rehiking a trail, studying the area, and looking for interesting facts, scenery, history, geology, and topography. I talked with a variety of hikers, asking them what they wanted a hike to cover and what made a "best hike." I had the best overall hiking region in Texas to choose from—central Texas, which includes the Edwards Plateau and the Hill Country.

I used the following criteria to come up with the best hikes included in this guide: accessibility, fun, exercise, family experience, scenery, history, rivers and lakes, experience of the hiker, moderate length (approximately 2 to 4 miles), dog friendliness, and wheelchair accessibility. Loops and preferably interconnecting loop trails were selected where possible, so a "best" hike within a park could be fashioned by combining the best of several trails.

Determining the "best" hikes in the area was a combination of personal judgment about whom the hike would appeal to and information from park staff and other hikers. Four of my favorite hikes are in the following parks: Wild Basin Wilderness, McKinney Roughs, Bastrop State Park, and Southeast Metro.

Trails are no longer the exclusive domain of the solitude-loving wilderness seeker or the dedicated fitness enthusiast. Whether providing recreational and educational opportunities, encouraging well-being, exploring history and geology, or bringing together people of all ages, hiking has become an important factor in many people's lives. I hope that at least some of these hikes will become your best hikes and that this book will be informative and interesting reading, as well as an excellent guide.

Austin Weather

The Austin climate is subtropical, with an average low temperature in January of 40°F and an average high in August of 96°F, followed closely by July at 95°F. The average yearly rainfall is 32 inches. The wettest month is May, averaging 5 inches. The driest month is January, with 1.9 inches of rain. The city generally has mild temperatures, with 300 days of sunshine a year.

State Parks Pass

For the best deal around, take advantage of the State Parks Pass. Instead of requiring you to pay on a per person/per visit basis, the pass provides entry to all ninety-three state parks for the member and all occupants of his or her vehicle. It's good for one year from time of purchase. It is available at most state parks and historic sites, as well as through the Customer Service Center in Austin (512-389-8900).

Flora and Fauna

The hiking trails around Austin, including portions of the

Texas Hill Country, have a biodiversity hard to equal. The area merges four major ecoregions—the post oak savanna, the blackland prairie, the south Texas plains, and the Edwards Plateau. Also, the Central Flyway, one of four major bird migration routes in the United States, is directly over the area. More than 400 of the 600 bird species recorded in the state have been seen in this region.

Most mammals are active during the night, so seeing them can be difficult. Look for their tracks around the trails and near streams or lakes. The Texas Parks & Wildlife Department has developed a series of nature trails, including the Great Texas Birding Trail–Central Coast and the Heart of Texas Wildlife Trail–East. Maps and location markers at the various sites reference areas where wildlife can be seen.

Some trees and plants native to east Texas—the "Lost Pines" in Bastrop State Park, for example—meet those of west Texas in transitional zones. Rivers and creeks are lined with bald cypress, black willow, hackberry, sycamore, cottonwood, and pecan. The upland areas contain a mix of deciduous and evergreen trees, including Ashe juniper, live oak, red oak, bigtooth maple, and Texas persimmon.

In spring and early summer, when wildflowers set the roadsides ablaze with color, driving to a hiking location can be a visual feast. Commonly seen are coreopsis (yellow), firewheels (red), phlox, Mexican hats, daisies, winecups (purple), yellow primrose, bluestem grass, and prickly pear cactus. The Texas bluebonnet, the state flower, is at its peak in late March and early April.

The diversity of wildflowers attracts many butterfly species, including the monarch, the state insect. The great ecological diversity of the territory, along with the flora and fauna, allows trips to be fashioned that are much more than just "a hike in the woods."

Zero Impact and Trail Etiquette

We have a responsibility to protect, no longer just conquer and use, our wild places. Many public hiking locations are at risk, so please do what you can to use them wisely. The following section will help you understand better what it means to take care of parks and wild places while still making the most of your hiking experience. Anyone can take a hike, but hiking safely and with good conservation practices is an art requiring preparation and proper equipment. Always leave an area as good as—or preferably better than—you found it.

- **Stay on the trail.** It's true, a path anywhere leads nowhere new, but purists will just have to get over it. Paths serve an important purpose: They limit impact on natural areas. Straying from a designated trail can cause damage to sensitive areas—damage that may take areas years to recover from, if they can recover at all. Even simple shortcuts can be destructive. Many of the hikes described in this guide are on or near areas ecologically important to supporting endangered flora and fauna. So, please, stay on the trail.

- **Leave no weeds.** Noxious weeds tend to overtake other plants, which in turn affects animals and birds that depend on them for food. To minimize the spread of noxious weeds, hikers should regularly clean their boots and hiking poles of mud and seeds. Nonnative invasive plants are particularly destructive and can quickly destroy acres of habitat. Yaupon is an example. Brush your dog to remove any weed seeds before heading off into a new area. Keep your dog under control. Always obey leash laws and be sure to bury your dog's waste or pack it out in resealable plastic bags.

- **Respect other trail users.** Often you're not the only one on the trail. With the rise in popularity of multiuse trails, you'll have to learn a new kind of respect, beyond the nod and "hello" approach of the past. First, investigate whether you're on a multiuse trail and take the appropriate precautions.

  For example, if you'll be sharing a trail with mountain bikers, you may not hear them coming—they can be like stealth airplanes. Bikers should always yield to hikers, but that's little comfort to the hiker. Be aware and stay to the right.

  More trails are being designed to be, at least in part, wheelchair accessible, so if you'll be using this type of trail, always step to the side to allow folks in wheelchairs time to navigate the terrain. Make them aware if you are going to pass around them.

First Aid

Sunburn

Take along sunscreen or sunblock, protective clothing, and a wide-brimmed hat. If you do get a sunburn, protect the area from further sun exposure. Remember that your eyes and lips are vulnerable to damaging radiation as well.

Blisters

Be prepared to take care of these hike-spoilers by carrying moleskin (a lightly padded adhesive) or gauze and tape. An effective way to apply moleskin is to cut out a circle of it, remove the center—like a doughnut—and place it over the blistered area.

Insect Bites and Stings

You can treat most insect bites and stings by taking a pain medication of your choice to reduce swelling. If you forgot to pack these items, a cold compress can sometimes ease the itching and discomfort. Don't pinch the area, as you'll only spread the venom.

Ticks

Ticks can carry diseases such as Rocky Mountain spotted fever and Lyme disease. The best defense is, of course, prevention. If you know you're going to be hiking through an area containing ticks, wear long pants and a long-sleeved shirt. At the end of your hike, do a spot check for ticks (and insects in general).

Poison Ivy, Oak, and Sumac

These skin irritants are prevalent on many of the trails in east Texas, sometimes growing into the trail. They come in the form of a bush or a vine, having leaflets in groups of three (poison ivy and oak), five, seven, or nine. Learn how to spot the plants, and especially show young children what to look for. Few things can spoil a hike, or your life the week after, more than accidentally getting poison ivy. The allergic reaction, in the form of blisters, usually occurs about twelve hours after exposure.

The best defense against these irritants is to wear clothing that covers the arms, legs, and torso. If you think you have come in contact with the plants, wash with soap and water after hiking. If the rash spreads, either tough it out or see your doctor.

Natural Hazards

Besides tripping over a rock or tree root on the trail, there are some real hazards to be aware of while hiking, including a few weather conditions you may need to take into account.

Lightning

Thunderstorms build over some areas in eastern Texas almost every day during the summer. Lightning can strike without warning, even several miles away from the nearest cloud. If you hear a buzzing or feel your hair standing on end, move quickly, as an electrical charge is building up.

The National Weather Service provides these cautions:

- If you can hear thunder, you are in striking distance of lightning.
- Suspend outdoor activities during thunderstorms and lightning.
- Get off high ground.
- Do not stay under trees.
- Get into an enclosed building or enclosed vehicle.

Now prepare for your next hike, remembering our responsibilities as modern-day hikers to do our part in conserving the outdoors. Enjoy.

How to Use This Guide

Twenty hikes are detailed in this guide. The overview map at the beginning of this guide shows the location of each hike in the area by hike number, keyed to the table of contents.

Each hike is accompanied by a route map that shows all the accessible roads and trails, points of interest, access to water, towns, landmarks, and geographical features. It also distinguishes trails from roads and paved roads from unpaved roads. The selected route is highlighted, and directional arrows point the way.

To aid in quick decision making, each hike begins with a summary to give you a taste of the hiking adventure to follow. You'll learn about the trail terrain and what surprises the route has to offer.

Next you'll find the quick, nitty-gritty details of the hike: hike length, approximate hiking time, difficulty rating, type of trail surface, best time of year to hike the trail, other trail users, canine compatibility, land status, fees and permits, trail hours, map resources, trail contacts, and other information that will help you on your trek.

Finding the trailhead provides directions from a nearby city or town right to where you'll want to park your car.

The Hike is the meat of the chapter. Detailed and honest, it's a carefully researched impression of the trail. While it's impossible to cover everything, you can rest assured that you won't miss what's important.

Miles and Directions provides mileage cues that identify all turns and trail name changes, as well as points of interest.

Don't feel restricted to the routes and trails mapped in this guide. Be adventurous and use the book as a platform to discover new routes for yourself, but do stick to designated trails. One of the simplest ways to begin is to turn the map upside down and hike the trail in reverse. The change in perspective can make the hike feel quite different; it's like getting two hikes for one.

You may wish to copy the directions for the course onto a small sheet to help you while hiking, or photocopy the map and cue sheet to take with you. Otherwise, just slip the whole book in your pocket and take it with you. Enjoy your time in the outdoors, and remember: Pack out what you pack in.

Map Legend

══════35══════	Interstate Highway
──────79──────	U.S. Highway
──────71──────	State Highway
────── 152 ──────	Local Road
= = = = = = = :	Unpaved Road
▬▬▬▬▬▬▬▬▬	Featured Route
- - - - - - - - -	Trail
～～～～～～	River/Creek
⬭	Lake/Pond
▭ ▭ ▭	Local Park/Golf Course
⏝	Bridge
▲	Campground
∧	Cave/Cavern
•—•	Gate
🅿	Parking
⛲	Picnic Area
■	Point of Interest/Structure
🚻	Restroom
⚕	Stable
○	Town
⓫	Trailhead
❓	Visitor/Information Center
▥	Viewpoint/Overlook
≋	Waterfall

1 Dove Springs

This is a hike for solitude and "roughing it" a bit. After a short walk along the tennis courts, the trail leads into the dense woods. Williamson Creek borders the south and east side of the hike. Sometimes following the trail can be a challenge.

Distance: 1.6-mile counterclockwise loop

Approximate hiking time: 1 hour

Difficulty: Easy (due to flat terrain and shade)

Trail surface: Crushed gravel and dirt

Best season: Year-round

Other trail users: Dog walkers, joggers, bikers on first 100 yards

Canine compatibility: Leashed dogs permitted

Land status: District park; City of Austin Parks Department

Fees and permits: None

Schedule: 5:00 a.m. to 10:00 p.m daily.

Maps: No maps available in the park. Map available at: www.ci .austin.tx.us/parks. USGS topo: Montopolis 7.5' quad

Trail contacts: Austin Parks and Recreation Department, 1600 City Park Rd., Austin 78730; (512) 346-3807 or (512) 974-6700

Finding the trailhead: From south Austin, take Montopolis Drive south from where it joins East Ben White Boulevard (TX 71). After 0.5 mile Montopolis Drive turns into East Stasney Lane after it crosses Burleson Road. Continue on East Stasney for 1.8 miles to Nuckols Road. Turn left at Nuckols Road and go to Palo Blanco Lane. Turn left onto Palo Blanco Lane and proceed to Ainez Drive. Turn into the community center, at 5801 Ainez Dr. Park adjacent to the tennis courts. *DeLorme: Texas Atlas & Gazetteer:* Page 69 G11. GPS: N30 11.186' / W97 44.345'

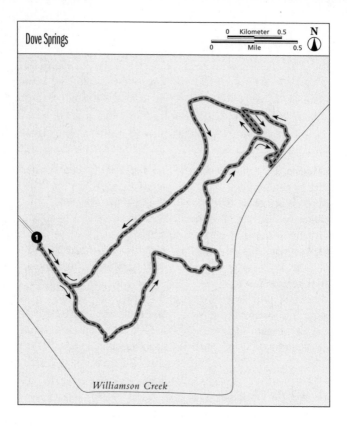

The Hike

This hike starts near the tennis courts and goes past the ball fields. It joins the paved jogging trail, which circles the play fields and has no shade. Follow the paved trail south into the wooded area, where the surface is dirt and grass. There is no trail signage, so keep heading generally south and east on the narrow path. The woods are heavy, and the undergrowth can be thick.

Walking becomes a little more difficult due to the undergrowth and the wandering nature of the trail. Birds can be heard and seen in the live oak and other trees, and Williamson Creek can be seen from the eastern sections. Portions of the eastern creek bank consist of rock and stone about 6 feet high.

Depending on the time of year and amount of rainfall, the creek can be slow moving and almost appear stagnant. The scene is entirely different after some rain, however. Small springs appear in the rock wall, and the water is crystal clear. There is a graveled area along the west side of the creek that affords the opportunity to sit and relax, enjoy the solitude, and possibly have a snack.

Part of the trail overlooks the creek and forest, while other sections are in the open or along the tree line. Hikers have created a number of paths and intersections that join the main trail, and at times these can be confusing. The final section of the hike is along the jogging trail.

Miles and Directions

0.0 Start at the trailhead near Ainez Drive and the basketball court. The trail is paved.

0.2 Follow the path to the right, heading southeast into the woods. The joggers' path goes left around the ball field.

0.3 Reach a Y and take the left branch, heading north.

0.4 Follow the trail as it zigzags a bit. Pass a path that comes in from the right (east), and then make a hard right, heading east.

0.5 Reach a T and take the right branch, still bearing east. Go down a stairway, bear left, and reach Williamson Creek. Turn left at the creek and follow it a short way, then go up a short but steep grade.

0.6 Follow the path west, away from the creek, and reach a T. Take the right branch, heading north. A playing field is on the left, up a 40-foot slope.

0.7 Go up about 25 steps, and at the top reach a Y. Take the right branch, heading slightly east.

0.75 Reach a T, and take the right branch, heading east. Go down a steep slope for about 15 feet to a grassy field and jogging trail. To shorten the hike, take the left branch and follow the jogging trail back to the parking area.

0.9 Bear slightly left, then right, to get to the bank of Williamson Creek. The creek is on the left.

1.1 Reach the jogging path and turn left, heading south.

1.2 Pass a baseball field on the right, surrounded by a chain-link fence.

1.3 Cross a concrete bridge about 25 feet long, going over a drainage ditch. A path from the hiking trail intersects from the left (east).

1.4 Follow the jogging trail curving to the right where the hiking trail intersects from the left side. Backtrack to the trailhead.

1.6 Arrive back at the trailhead.

2 Southeast Metropolitan Park: Primitive Trail

Hiking nearly 3 miles up, down, and around the backbone of a ridge, with forest, cactus, and undergrowth reaching to the trail's edge, makes this feel like the wilderness. Two ponds offer resting points on their fishing piers. Downtown Austin can be seen from one of the overlooks. This is acknowledged as the best hike in eastern Travis County.

Distance: 2.6-mile loop

Approximate hiking time: 1.75 hours

Difficulty: Moderate (due to some steep inclines up the ridge)

Trail surface: Gravel, dirt path

Best season: Year-round

Other trail users: Joggers, dog walkers

Canine compatibility: Leashed dogs permitted

Land status: Travis County park

Fees and permits: None

Schedule: Open 8:00 a.m. to 9:00 p.m. May 1 to September 15. Opens at 9:00 a.m. rest of year. Closes at 7:30 p.m. March 2 to October 31, at 6:00 p.m. November 1 to March 1

Maps: A large map is mounted on the board at the trailhead. NCGS topo: Webberville, 7.5' quad

Trail contacts: Travis County Park Department, 1010 Lavaca St., Austin 78701; (512) 854-7275

Finding the trailhead: From Austin, take I-35 to TX 71 and head east. Go past Austin-Bergstrom International Airport, and look for the park on the left about 2 miles beyond. There are signs along TX 71. After entering the park, veer to the right and follow the signs indicating a hiking trail all the way back to the parking area next to the trailhead. *DeLorme: Texas Atlas & Gazetteer:* Page 69 G11. GPS: N30 11.658' / W97 36.570'

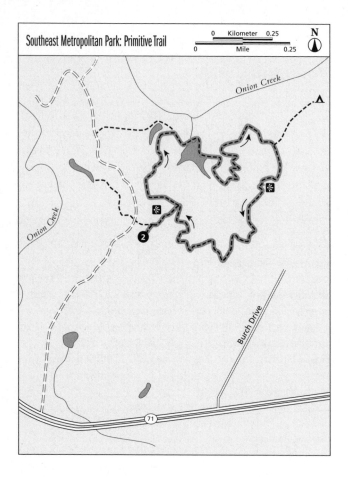

Southeast Metropolitan Park: Primitive Trail

Onion Creek

Onion Creek

Burch Drive

71

The Hike

Start on the Primitive Trail, reputed to be the best in the southeast Austin area. No maps are available, but there is a large map board at the trailhead. Head northeast, following along the backbone of the ridge and quickly come to trail marker 1, with a sign pointing to the left stating WILDLIFE VIEWING BLIND.

Continue straight, around cedars, oaks, and prickly pear cactus, the state plant. A wide set of wooden stairs leads to a scenic overlook that on a clear day includes a glimpse of downtown Austin. Almost immediately beyond the overlook, you'll come to the intersection of the east and west branches of the Primitive Trail. Take the left branch, going west. Butterflies, dragonflies, and moths are numerous. Cross several dry streambeds and gullies; many have bridges. The trail meanders around, going up and down the steep ridgeline. A path on the left leads to an unnamed small pond. A pier reaches over the water, and catch-and-release fishing is allowed. Near the pond, the route splits: The left branch is a service road that loops back to the trailhead. Keep to the right, and another pond comes into view on the right; it has a covered fishing pier. There are some American beauty bushes with large quantities of small blue berries, a favorite food of wildlife. The soft bank around the ponds is a good place to look for animal and bird tracks.

Start bearing away from the pond at marker 18 and continue through a canyon and back up the ridge. This is the steepest section of the hike and is great cardiovascular exercise. Come to an overgrown path that intersects the trail on the left and leads to a primitive camping area. Some of the trail is single-track. Steps have been strategically placed to aid in ascending and descending the ridge. The trail heads down and follows the contours of the ridge to an intersection on the left. Take the left fork to the wildlife viewing blind sign and then turn right. This is a short out-and-back path that leads to the edge of a pond and the blind. Onion

Creek is to the southwest, but not visible. Return to the Primitive Trail and turn right to go the short distance back to the trailhead.

This hike, except for the trail markers and bridges, gives the feeling of being in the backcountry. Southeast Metropolitan Park also contains a 2-mile concrete, wheelchair-accessible, multiuse trail.

Miles and Directions

0.0 Start at the Primitive Trail trailhead adjacent to the parking area.

0.1 Reach a shelter. Go down the stairs and make a hard right turn.

0.2 Go down six steps to a wooden bridge crossing a gully about 25 feet wide.

0.3 Pass trail marker 8. Continue following the trail to the right.

0.5 Pass a covered fishing pier at the edge of a pond. Catch-and-release fishing is allowed.

0.6 A pond is on the right. Cross a concrete embankment to get to the trail. This walkway can be flooded after a heavy rain.

1.0 Bear left at trail marker 25, then cross a bridge over a gully.

1.4 Pass the group camping sign, near trail marker 35.

1.7 A bridge crosses a narrow gully.

2.0 Pass trail marker 48 and immediately go down three steps to cross another bridge. These bridges are an aid on the rough terrain. Follow the trail to the right after crossing the bridge.

2.2 Cross a bridge that is identified as number 5. This bridge goes over a dry creek bed.

2.5 Pass the wildlife viewing blind sign.

2.6 Arrive back at the trailhead.

3 McKinney Roughs Nature Park: Riverside Trails

This route combines the best of the 17 miles of McKinney Roughs Nature Park's crisscrossed collection of loops and out-and-back trails into one spectacular 2.5-mile hike. Start from the flat ridgetop, then head down to the Colorado River, getting sweeping views of rolling box canyons, steep ravines, juniper and oak forests, wildflower meadows, and the river itself. Pass through four Texas ecoregions: post oak savanna, blackland prairie, east Texas piney woods, and central Texas plateau.

Distance: 2.5-mile loop
Approximate hiking time: 1.75 hours
Difficulty: Moderate (due to easy grades)
Trail surface: Dirt path, sand
Best season: September to June
Other trail users: Equestrians, dog walkers
Canine compatibility: Leashed dogs permitted
Land status: Lower Colorado River Authority park
Fees and permits: Check in at the visitor center before hiking to pay the day-use fee and get a trail map and information. The fee includes the opportunity to borrow one of three nature packs:

Birding Pack, with binoculars and guidebook; Plant Pack, with magnifying glass and explanation of what plants to look for; Kid Pack, with bug containers and children's books describing the plants, birds, and insects found at the park.
Schedule: 8:00 a.m. to 5:00 p.m. daily; day use only
Maps: Trail maps are available in the park office and also on the Web site www.lcra.org/library/media/public/docs/community_mck_roughs_trailmap.pdf. NCGS topo: Utley, 7.5' quad
Trail contacts: McKinney Roughs Nature Park, 1884 TX 71 West, Cedar Creek 78612; (512) 303-5073

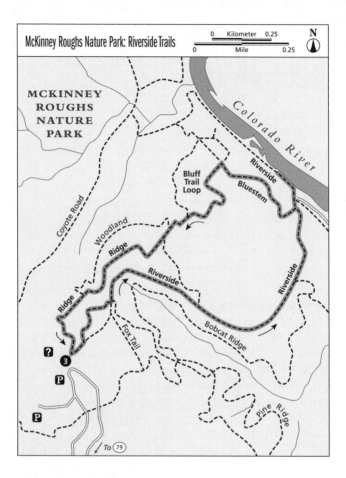

0   Kilometer   0.25   N

0   Mile   0.25

MCKINNEY
ROUGHS
NATURE
PARK

Colorado River

Bluff
Trail
Loop

Riverside

Bluestem

Coyote Road

Woodland

Ridge

Riverside

Ridge

Riverside

Fox Tail

Bobcat Ridge

? 3

P

Pine Ridge

P

To 79

Finding the trailhead: From Austin, head east on TX 71 past Austin-Bergstrom International Airport. Proceed for about 13 miles beyond the airport, and look for the park's distinctive rock-wall entrance with a windmill on the left (north). Hikers should check in at the Lower Colorado River Authority (LCRA) office near the main parking area. The main hiking trailhead is behind the Environmental Learning Center adjacent to

the main parking lot. *DeLorme: Texas Atlas & Gazetteer:* Page 69 G11.
GPS: N30 11' 653" W97 36' 572"

The Hike

To begin, head north toward the Colorado River, about a mile away. As the trail descends into the bottomlands of the river, the higher plateau rises on each side. The tree cover consists of a combination of cedar and oak, with clumps of low-growing cactus growing under the cedars.

Several trails intercept the Riverside Trail, including Fox Tail, Pine Ridge, Valley View, Bobcat Ridge, Bluestem, and Cypress. A number of these are short connector trails to the major loop trails. This gives you the capability to shorten or lengthen the route on the go. All the trails have signs that point back to the headquarters. This is handy if the hike has been altered, as it keeps you oriented as to whether you're coming or going. The trail narrows, some sections being single-track. The ground is covered with various grasses and an abundance of poison ivy. Riverside Trail is shared with equestrians.

Upon reaching the river, continue for about a quarter mile northwest on a short out-and-back path to see the various types of vegetation and signs of animals, especially their tracks. This can be fun and adds another dimension to the hike. Backtrack to the junction with the Bluestem Trail, turn right onto Bluestem, and proceed to where the Bluff Trail Loop crosses it. There are some zigs and zags with some steep sections. Turn left onto the east section of Bluff Trail Loop. There are several lookout points where you can view the Colorado River. Continue around the loop to where Ridge Trail runs into it. Turn left onto Ridge Trail, which has a surface of packed gravel, making it wheelchair accessible. Interpretive signs placed by local Boy Scout troops describe the various flowers seen in the meadows. There are several sweeping overlooks into a box canyon below. This is not a conventional box canyon with three sides bordered by high walls; instead it is a rolling canyon about 90 feet deep, with no obvious entrance.

In May it's possible to see flocks, called "waves," of warblers. The yellow-rumped warbler, with a distinctive lemon-yellow patch above its tail and on its side, is one of the most common. Pass both junctions with the Woodland connector loop, then bend left to get back to the trailhead. Greater roadrunners (beep! beep!), running along with their tails pointing upward just like in the cartoons, are resident birds. Cowboys called the roadrunner the "chaparral cock." McKinney Roughs Nature Park contains the most extensive collection of varied hiking trails in central Texas.

Miles and Directions

0.0 Start at the Riverside Trail trailhead behind the Environmental Learning Center building.

0.1 On the right (north), Fox Tail and Pine Ridge Trails intersect and end at Riverside Trail. Continue on Riverside Trail as it bends left.

0.3 On the left (north), Valley View Trail intersects and ends at Riverside Trail. Continue forward (southeast), and then bear left on Riverside Trail.

0.7 On the right (east), Bobcat Ridge Trail intersects and ends at Riverside Trail. Continue by bearing left (north) on Riverside Trail.

0.9 On the left (west), Bluestem Trail intersects and ends at Riverside Trail, and on the right (east), Cypress Trail intersects and ends at Riverside Trail. Bend left (north) and quickly bear left (northeast) on Riverside Trail. The Colorado River is in view on the right. Hike along the Colorado River for about 0.25 mile, and then backtrack to the intersection with Bluestem Trail.

1.4 Turn right at the intersection with Bluestem Trail and continue northwest to the T intersection with Bluff Trail Loop.

1.5 Take the left fork onto the Bluff Trail Loop, heading south. Cross some dry streambeds.

1.8 Pass the western leg of the Bluff Trail Loop on the right. Continue to where the Ridge Trail intersects with the Bluff Trail Loop. Continue on the Ridge Trail, which is packed gravel and wheelchair accessible. Some outcroppings of limestone are on the trail. On the right, the north section of Woodland Trail intersects and ends at Ridge Trail.

2.2 On the right, the south section of Woodland Trail intersects and ends at Ridge Trail. Continue heading south on Ridge Trail.

2.5 End the hike back at the trailhead by the Environmental Learning Center.

4 McKinney Roughs Nature Park: Buckeye Trail

It's always great to find a new trail, such as the Buckeye Trail in McKinney Roughs Nature Park qualifies, which opened in late 2007. This is really a connector trail between the Road Runner Trail and the Pecan Bottom Trail, making those trails easier to reach. Buckeye Trail passes through the post oak/blackjack oak savanna ecosystem and leads to one of the largest pecan trees in the state.

Distance: 3-mile loop
Approximate hiking time: 1.5 hours
Difficulty: Moderate (due to easy grades)
Trail surface: Dirt path, sand
Best season: September to June
Other trail users: Equestrians, dog walkers
Canine compatibility: Leashed dogs permitted
Land status: Lower Colorado River Authority park
Fees and permits: Check in at the visitor center before hiking to pay the day-use fee and get a trail map and information. Fee includes the opportunity to borrow one of three nature packs: Birding Pack, with binoculars and guidebook; Plant Pack, with magnifying glass and explanation of what plants to look for; Kid Pack, with bug containers and children's books describing the plants, birds, and insects found at the park.
Schedule: 8:00 a.m. to 5:00 p.m. daily; day use only
Maps: Trail maps are available in the park office and also on the Web site www.lcra.org/library/media/public/docs/community_mck_roughs_trailmap.pdf. NCGS topo: Utley, 7.5' quad
Trail contacts: McKinney Roughs Nature Park, 1884 TX 71 West, Cedar Creek 78612; (512) 303-5073

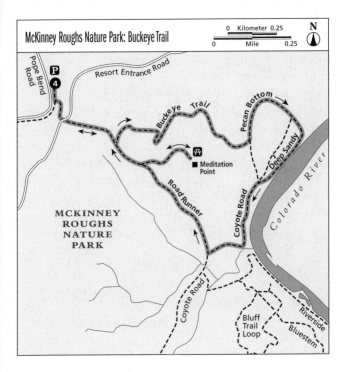

Buckeye Trail

Pecan Bottom

Deep Sandy

Meditation Point

Road Runner

Colorado River

Resort Entrance Road

Pope Bend Road

MCKINNEY ROUGHS NATURE PARK

Coyote Road

Coyote Road

Bluff Trail Loop

Bluestem

Riverside

0   Kilometer   0.25
0   Mile   0.25

N

Finding the trailhead: From Austin, head east on TX 71 past Austin-Bergstrom International Airport. Proceed for about 13 miles beyond the airport and look for the park's rock-wall entrance with a windmill on the left (north). Hikers should check in at the Lower Colorado River Authority (LCRA) office near the main parking area. The Buckeye trailhead is located at the Pope Bend Equestrian Trail parking area, across the road leading to the Hyatt Regency Resort. From park headquarters, drive to the park entrance and turn right (northwest) onto TX 71, continue less than a mile, and turn right (north) onto Pope Bend Road. Proceed for about a mile to the Pope Bend Equestrian Trailhead parking lot, on your right. *DeLorme: Texas Atlas & Gazetteer:* Page 69 G11. GPS: N30 92.700' / W97 27.484'

The Hike

This hike combines sections of the Buckeye, Road Runner, Coyote Road, Deep Sandy, and Pecan Bottom Trails. Legend has it that bandits used this remote area as a hideout. Start at the Pope Bend Equestrian Trailhead on the northwest side of McKinney Roughs Nature Park.

Follow the Road Runner Trail to the Buckeye Trail and turn left. Enter the woods, which contain several species of oak trees and are part of the post oak savanna ecosystem. Bear east on the Buckeye Trail, passing a box canyon to the right. The trail is shared by equestrians, so use caution.

A visual feast of wildflowers greets the hiker along many trails. During May, the woods are full of North America's prettiest birds, the warblers. Seeing a flock of these, containing several species and hundreds of birds, is spectacular. One of the more conspicuous is the yellow warbler, which is the only all-yellow warbler, making it easy to spot and identify.

The Buckeye Trail descends until it ends at an intersection with the Pecan Bottom Trail. After making a sweeping right bend and heading southeast, you will see a huge pecan tree. It's impressive and it would probably take three men with outstretched arms to circle the trunk. There is a picnic table located nearby where you can rest in the shade. Continue on down toward the Colorado River, passing Coyote Road on the right. Pecan Bottom ends as it merges into Deep Sandy Trail. Bear southwest, walking along the river, where the scenery is totally different from that of the uplands. The forest has been replaced by the river's flat bottomland and lush growth of bushes and grasses. The river's edge is a good place to look for animal signs, including tracks. After about one-third of a mile, Deep Sandy Trail ends where it merges into Coyote Road. Take the left branch, heading south along the river's edge. Watch for poison ivy. Bend right and head away from the river. At the intersection with Road Runner Trail, turn right and head up into the woods. Look to the left to see some small peaky hills, which are called knobs. The most famous knob in the area is Pilot Knob, the remains of an extinct volcano. Take the spur on the right to a scenic overlook called Meditation Point. The panorama includes a box canyon and the best view of the Colorado River in the park. There are picnic tables, and this is a nice place to rest or have a snack. Return to the Road Runner Trail, go past the branch with the Buckeye Trail, and then backtrack to the trailhead.

Miles and Directions

0.0 Start at the Road Runner trailhead, following the Road Runner Trail to the Buckeye Trail.

0.1 Pass the intersection (actually less than 100 yards) with the Yaupon Trail on the right (Yaupon Trail heads south). Continue straight, heading east on the Road Runner Trail. The Buckeye connector trail intersects the Road Runner Trail on the left (northeast). Turn left onto the Buckeye Trail, following the contours of the hills.

0.6 The Buckeye Trail ends at the Pecan Bottom Trail. Turn left, heading north and walking in the Colorado River lowlands.

0.9 Pass Coyote Road on the right (south) where it intersects the Pecan Bottom Trail.

1.0 Pecan Bottom Trail merges into the Deep Sandy connector to Coyote Road.

1.3 Deep Sandy Trail merges into Coyote Road. Continue left, heading south on Coyote Road, with the Colorado River on the left (east). Also at this junction, Coyote Road runs north and south, and the Pecan Bottom Trail connects to Coyote Road from the right (north).

1.8 Travel close to the river. Make a right turn, heading west and away from the river bottomland, and begin to climb the slopes. Come to a junction with the Road Runner Trail. Turn right (northwest) onto the Road Runner Trail. Coyote Road continues southwest.

2.3 There is a spur on the right (northeast) that leads to Meditation Point. Take the spur. This leads to an overlook that furnishes the best view in the park of the Colorado River. Several picnic benches are located here. Backtrack to the Road Runner Trail.

2.8 Turn right (northwest) where the spur intersects the Road Runner Trail.

2.9 Pass the intersection on the right (northeast) where the Buckeye connector trail joins the Road Runner Trail. Continue west, backtracking on the Road Runner Trail to the trailhead.

3.0 Arrive back at the trailhead.

5 McKinney Falls State Park: Homestead Trail

The walk to get to the trailhead is a miniadventure. Go over the lavalike rock flows from Pilot Knob volcano, which created Lower McKinney Falls eighty million years ago. Then ford Onion Creek, or wade across the top of the falls. The trail passes by the ruins of Thomas F. McKinney's 1850s homestead and grist mill. Return to the trailhead and walk to the Smith Rock Shelter Trail to view the remnants of a natural rock shelter used hundreds of years ago.

Distance: 3-mile loop
Approximate hiking time: 1.5 hours
Difficulty: Moderate (due to a slight elevation gain and a rocky outcrop)
Trail surface: Dirt path with some limestone outcrops
Best season: September to June
Other trail users: Mountain bikers, joggers, dog walkers
Canine compatibility: Leashed dogs permitted
Land status: State park; Texas Parks & Wildlife Department
Fees and permits: Day-use fee (or use the State Parks Pass)
Schedule: 8:00 a.m. to 10:00 p.m. daily
Maps: Trail maps are available in the park office. You can also find maps on the Web site www.tpwd .state.tx.us. NCGS topo: Montopolis, 7.5' quad
Trail contacts: McKinney Falls State Park, 5808 McKinney Falls Pkwy., Austin 78744; (512) 243-1643

Finding the trailhead: From Austin, head south on US 183, passing the junctions with US 290 and TX 71. After passing TX 71, Austin-Bergstrom Airport is on the left (east). McKinney Falls Parkway is on the right (west). There is a brown state park sign that marks the turn. McKinney Falls State Park is about 3 miles from the turn, on the

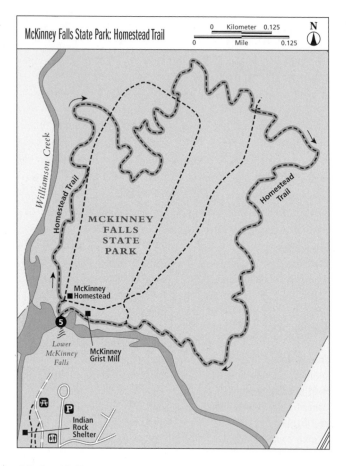

McKinney Falls State Park: Homestead Trail

0 Kilometer 0.125
0 Mile 0.125

N

Williamson Creek

Homestead Trail

Homestead Trail

MCKINNEY
FALLS
STATE
PARK

McKinney
Homestead

5

Lower McKinney Falls

McKinney
Grist Mill

P

Indian
Rock
Shelter

right (north). Enter the park and drive to the park headquarters. Leave the headquarters and take a right, following the park road. Turn right to the Lower McKinney Falls parking area. From here, walk down to the creek and waterfall area. After crossing Onion Creek at the Lower Falls, the trailhead is to the right and marked HOMESTEAD TRAIL. *DeLorme: Texas Atlas & Gazetteer:* Page 69 G11. GPS: N30 11.172' / W97 43.26'

The Hike

To start, head left from the parking area, following the northern section of the loop. The trail follows portions of Williamson Creek and Onion Creek; both are important wildlife corridors. Water snakes, including venomous water moccasins, may be near the water's edge. Be careful.

Bear left toward the remains of the Thomas F. McKinney two-story home. The park is named after McKinney, who settled here in the 1850s and was one of the original 300 colonists in Stephen F. Austin's early-nineteenth-century settlement. Follow the trail as it makes a few turns and then runs parallel with Williamson Creek. Bald cypress, sycamore, buttonbush, and willow trees line the creek bank. The trail is narrow but easy to follow and has thick undergrowth at the edges, where poison ivy can be abundant. Bend hard right, going south and away from the creek. The Texas Parks & Wildlife Department's headquarters complex can be seen to the left.

Watch for large spider webs woven across the path by orb weavers, a common garden spider. In the summer the throaty sound of "chic-breee" may be heard. This is the call of the summer tanager, the only entirely red bird in North America. The park is located at the junction of the Edwards Plateau and the blackland prairie, with the resulting mixed habitats, and is home to 224 species of birds and many mammals. Follow the trail down and across a dry wash and through a large stand of oaks, where the trail crosses a long open stretch of bedrock. Sometimes the limestone forms a stair-stepping topography with sharp drop-offs to the creek.

The stabilized remains of the McKinney grist mill now come into view. This was the first mill in the area and was a major contributor to the economy.

In August great egrets can be seen roosting high in the cypress trees, while great blue herons feed along the creek banks. The terrain leading to Lower Falls was formed eighty million years ago by the eruptions of Pilot Knob volcano. Backtrack across the Lower Falls and the limestone moonscape back to the parking lot.

After the hike, enjoy the picnic area along Onion Creek. Visit the Smith Rock Shelter Trail, where Native Americans roamed hundreds of years ago. The 3.5-mile Onion Creek Hike and Bike Trail loop is also in the park and is wheelchair accessible. The park, although located only 13 miles south of Austin, retains a rustic, out-in-the-woods atmosphere.

Miles and Directions

0.0 Start the Homestead Trail after crossing Onion Creek, then continue to the left, heading north.

0.4 Reach the McKinney Homestead, which is partly hidden by trees. Williamson Creek is on the left (west) and the park maintenance road is on the right (east), but it cannot be seen from the trail.

1.1 Cross the park maintenance road and continue heading east.

1.3 Cross the park maintenance road heading north, and then the trail twists and turns and veers sharply right, heading east.

1.5 Go past the park maintenance road junction on the right and continue heading east.

2.3 Veer hard right, heading south.

2.8 Reach the remains of the McKinney grist mill. Continue past the mill back to the trailhead and cross the Lower Falls.

3.0 Arrive back at the parking area.

6 Circle C Ranch: Slaughter Creek

Interest is added to the hike as it passes by a fenced area that protects a karst cave. A karst is an underground area of eroded limestone, caves, and streams, and the karst under central Texas allows groundwater to flow into the Edwards Aquifer. Cross Slaughter Creek twice, once over a concrete path and the second time by using rocks as stepping stones. The loop around the soccer fields is an easy hike that's good for families with young children.

Distance: 2.4-mile counterclockwise loop
Approximate hiking time: 1.5 hours
Difficulty: Moderate (due to 100 yards of rough rocky terrain)
Trail surface: Crushed granite
Best season: Year-round
Other trail users: Dog walkers, joggers, bikers, parents with strollers
Canine compatibility: Leashed dogs permitted
Land status: Metro park; City of

Austin Parks Department
Fees and permits: None
Schedule: Daily, dawn to dusk. Entrance gate is locked when the park closes.
Maps: No maps available in the park. Visit the Web site www.ci .austin.tx.us/parks/traildirectory .htm for maps. NCGS topo: Signal Hill, 7.5' quad
Trail contacts: Austin Parks and Recreation Department, 1600 City Park Rd., Austin 78730; (512) 346-3807 or (512) 974-6700

Finding the trailhead: From south Austin, take the MoPac Expressway south from William Cannon Drive for 2.5 miles. Turn right at the West Slaughter Lane exit. Go west on Slaughter Lane for less than a mile. Pass Escarpment Boulevard and watch for the park entrance at 6301 West Slaughter La. Go to the west side of the most distant parking area. Park near the restrooms and water fountain. The

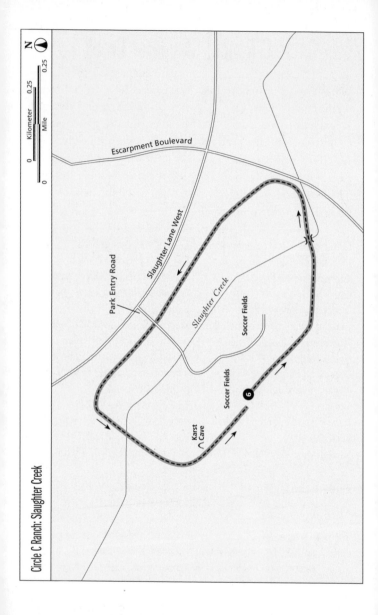

Circle C Ranch: Slaughter Creek

trailhead is directly behind the restroom building. *DeLorme: Texas Atlas & Gazetteer:* Page 69 G10. GPS: N30 11.975' / W97 53.215'

The Hike

Start from the southern trailhead directly behind the restroom building, near the west side of the farthest parking lot. Turn left onto the asphalt trail heading toward a soccer field and woods to the right. The trail circles around a large number of soccer fields. Follow the trail slightly southeast and continue to follow the loop left, in a counterclockwise direction.

Turn left near the path to the disc golf course, where the trail turns to packed gravel. Cedars, live oak, and other hardwood trees are about 30 feet from the trail's edge. Mourning doves and other birds are frequently seen. The right side of the trail slopes slightly up, while the left is flat, with some low limestone outcroppings. One section of the trail has 1- to 2-foot-diameter rocks separating the path from a soccer field. Reach a Y and take the left branch, heading east.

Walk under a tunnel formed by branches of live oak trees and reach a concrete crossing over Slaughter Creek. Depending upon the amount of rainfall, the creek may be flowing or just be a dry creek bed. On the left side, to the north, the creek branches around several large oak and syca-more trees. This presents a good photo op.

Follow the trail east for a short distance, and then bear left (north). Escarpment Boulevard is to the right (east) and Slaughter Lane is straight ahead (north). Veer slightly left, heading northwest, with Slaughter Lane paralleling the trail. Pass by two concrete benches on the left, next to a disc golf "hole," which is actually a concrete pad.

Reach an unpaved parking area near the park entrance and adjoining the park entrance road. Use caution and cross the road, heading northeast. Cedar and oak trees are about 30 feet off the trail, and depending on the season, this is a favorite section for butterflies.

Bend to the left and reach a T. Take the left branch, heading southwest. Utility lines and a fire hydrant are straight ahead. Here the trail is highly eroded and has many small rocks on it. This 100 yards is the most difficult section of the hike. The park boundary fence is to the right. Reach and cross Slaughter Creek, which may be flowing or dry depending on the amount of rain. The dry creek bed is about 35 feet wide, rough, with a limestone bottom and rocks strewn about.

Continue straight and pass a basketball court with a narrow dirt path leading to it. The trail changes to a dirt and grass path. Pass along a soccer field and turn left at the goal line, walking between woods on the right and the field on the left.

Miles and Directions

0.0 Start at the southern trailhead near the main parking area and behind the restrooms. There is no marked trailhead. Turn left, heading south onto the asphalt trail.

0.1 Turn left and head southeast at a disc golf pad.

0.2 Continue to follow the trail, bearing left and then straight. Pass a park maintenance path on the right.

0.4 Cross over a dirt road and bear left. Go straight, heading generally east.

0.5 Reach a Y and take the left branch, heading east.

0.6 Reach a concrete bridge crossing Slaughter Creek. Depending on the amount of rain, the creek can be a dry bed filled with rocks or a stream flowing over the concrete slab.

0.7 Continue to follow the trail and cross over a 3-foot-wide gravel path. About 60 yards straight ahead is Slaughter Lane. Just before the road is a short limestone block wall.

0.8 Continue to follow the trail to where it appears to dead-end. Escarpment Boulevard is to the east. Turn left where the trail restarts, heading north.

1.0 Follow the trail, bearing slightly left (northwest) and with Slaughter Lane to the right (northeast).

1.1 Reach a concrete section of the trail that's about 100 feet long.

1.3 Reach the park entrance road. Cross the entry road and stay on the trail, heading north. Use caution. Or follow the entrance road back to the parking area.

1.6 Continue to follow the trail, generally to the left and north-west. Reach a T and take the left branch, heading south-west. There are utility lines and a fire hydrant straight ahead.

1.7 The trail becomes highly eroded and rocky for about 100 yards. This is the most difficult part of the hike. Cross Slaughter Creek, which is about 35 feet wide.

1.8 Continue to follow the trail, with the park boundary fence and utility lines to the right, about 8 feet away. Pass a basketball court and soccer fields. The crushed gravel trail changes to dirt.

1.9 Turn left at the end of the soccer field and walk along the grass between the soccer field and the woods.

2.0 Follow the trail, bearing left (southeast), and pass a high fence on the left protecting a karst cave. A soccer field abuts the fence.

2.2 Bend hard left at a baseball field backstop fence and continue to follow the trail southeast.

2.3 Reach the disc golf pad and backtrack to the start of the trail.

2.4 Arrive back at the trailhead.

7 Dick Nichols

The loop trail is encircled by oak trees, shrubs, and good habitat for birds and other wildlife. The semiwild areas near the edges of the path invite investigation. Squirrels and raccoons may be seen during the day. This is an easy hike for beginners and families. It is wheelchair and stroller accessible.

Distance: 1.4-mile counterclockwise loop
Approximate hiking time: 1 hour
Difficulty: Easy (due to paved trail and flat terrain)
Trail surface: Paved concrete
Best season: Year-round
Other trail users: Dog walkers, joggers, bikers
Canine compatibility: Leashed dogs permitted
Land status: District park; City of Austin Parks Department

Fees and permits: None
Schedule: 5:00 a.m. to 10:00 p.m.
Maps: No maps available in the park; visit the Web site www.ci.austin.tx.us/parks/traildirectory.htm for maps. NCGS topo: Oak Hill, 7.5' quad
Trail contacts: Austin Parks and Recreation Department, 1600 City Park Rd., Austin 78730; (512) 346-3807 or (512) 974-6700

Finding the trailhead: From south Austin, get on the south MoPac Expressway at US 290. Head south for 1.2 miles and exit at William Cannon Drive. Head west on William Cannon Drive for 1.2 miles and take the Beckett Road exit. Follow Beckett Road south for about 1 mile and turn into the park entrance on the left, at 8011 Beckett Rd. The trailhead is near the west side of the parking area. *DeLorme: Texas Atlas & Gazetteer:* Page 69 G10. GPS: N30 12.533' / W97 51.450'

The Hike

This concrete-paved trail follows and is close to the park's

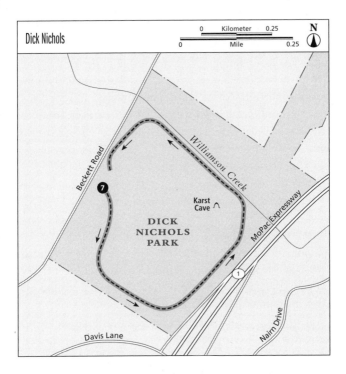

perimeter boundaries. Heavy woods border the outside edge of this 152-acre park. The counterclockwise loop first heads south, then east, then north, and finally west to complete the hike. The northwest section follows Williamson Creek, but the creek is hidden by woods. There is a portion on the south end that parallels the MoPac Expressway, and some road noise can be heard. The trail is wheelchair and stroller accessible.

A little farther than halfway into the hike, bear left, passing an exercise station, and then veer slightly to the right.

You'll see a 3-foot stone wall. A narrow dirt path to the right leads to it. The wall surrounds a wooded area with a large live oak in the middle. The purpose of the barrier wall is to protect a small karst cave. A karst is an underground area of eroded limestone, caves, and streams, and the karst under central Texas allows groundwater to flow into the Edwards Aquifer. This aquifer provides the city of Austin with its drinking water supply. This makes karst caves ecologically sensitive, so while good photo ops are available, *do not enter* the enclosed area.

Return to the trail, which has a good tree canopy of mostly cedars. Small groups of prickly pear cactus, the state plant, grow around the cedars. There are a number of small openings into the woods that have live oak trees shrouded with Spanish moss. Some of these openings have narrow dirt paths that invite exploration. The mostly flat ground has some small limestone rocks breaking the surface.

Depending on the season, butterflies flit back and forth across the trail. The woods and creek offer good habitat for numerous birds and small animals, including raccoon, opossum, and squirrel. This trail on the south side of Austin provides an easy and relaxing hike.

Miles and Directions

0.0 Start at the trailhead near the west side of the parking area and head south.

0.1 Pass a water fountain and tennis courts on the left. Continue to follow the trail straight (south).

0.2 Bend left and then right, and pass an exercise station on the left. Then bear southeast.

0.3 Pass a path intersecting the trail from the right. The path leads into the woods. Continue to follow the trail to the left (southeast). Utility lines and a short section of fence are on the right.

0.5 Pass paths that lead both right and left into the woods. Follow the trail, making a hard left and heading northeast.

0.7 Follow the trail, veering right and left, and then pass an exercise station on the left.

0.8 Pass a path to the right that leads about 100 feet to a 3-foot-high stone wall, surrounding a karst cave. Entry to the cave area is prohibited. Continue to follow the trail due north.

0.9 Bear left, going northwest. Williamson Creek is to the right, but it's hidden by the woods.

1.1 Pass a path on the left that leads to a playing field, and then bear slightly left, heading northwest. There is an exercise station on the left, and the parking area comes into view.

1.3 Tennis courts are on the left, and a drainage retention pond abuts them. Bear to the left, toward the parking area.

1.4 End the hike at the parking area.

8 Goat Cave: Karst Preserve Trail

This hike, which allows you to see a small section of the underground karst world, is a great hike for young children or others interested in learning more about the Edwards Aquifer and the geology around Austin. Several small caves have been formed here by the collapse of sinkholes. Goat Cave, near the end of the hike, is home to a colony of bats. Entry is prohibited.

Distance: 0.7 mile out and back
Approximate hiking time: 0.75 hour
Difficulty: Easy (due to flat terrain and short distance)
Trail surface: Dirt with some rock
Best season: Year-round
Other trail users: Bird-watchers
Canine compatibility: Dogs not permitted
Land status: Nature preserve; City of Austin Parks Department
Fees and permits: None

Schedule: Dawn to dusk; day use only
Maps: No maps available in the park; visit the Web site www.ci .austin.tx.us/parks/traildirectory .htm for maps. NCGS topo: Oak Hill, 7.5' quad
Trail contacts: Austin Parks and Recreation Department, 1600 City Park Rd., Austin 78730; (512) 346-3807 or (512) 974-6700
Special considerations: No bikes permitted

Finding the trailhead: From south Austin, take Capital of Texas Highway south to the Lamar Boulevard exit. Follow Lamar Boulevard for 1.4 miles to the Brodie Lane exit. Follow Brodie Lane south for 3 miles to Deer Lane. Turn right (west) onto Deer Lane; the preserve is on the right at 3900 Deer La. Park along the wide shoulder on the north side of the road at the preserve entrance. This is a public road, so be sure to take any valuables with you and lock your vehicle. *DeLorme: Texas Atlas & Gazetteer:* Page 69 G10. GPS: N30 11.814' / W97 50.884'

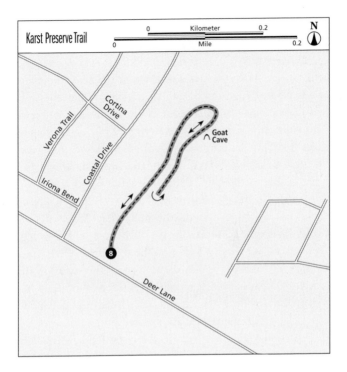

The Hike

At the trailhead, stop at the kiosk to read about karst geology and cave inhabitants, including troglobites, troglozenes, and troglophiles. Several endangered species make these caves their home. All are adapted to living in a wet, humid, constant-temperature environment, and some have no eyes. Some are so small that it is difficult to see them without using magnification. Larger animals, spiders, snakes, and bats also use the sinkholes. Karsts are formed when slightly acidic water percolates down through soluble rocks, mostly limestone, creating sinkholes and caves.

The trail is dirt, mostly shaded and flat. Live oak trees and other species cover the entire eight-acre preserve, providing ample shade. Three sinkholes—Wade Sink, Hide Out Sink, and Goat Cave—can be viewed from paths leading to them. This entire area is ecologically sensitive, so stay on the trail or paths, and do not climb on, or attempt to explore, the caves.

Start to follow the trail north, and in less than 500 feet a path leads to the left. Wade Sink is about 30 feet down the path. The hole is 8 feet by 15 feet in diameter, with rocks and slab rock around the perimeter. After carefully exploring the area, return to the main trail and turn left. Residences and Coastal Drive can be seen through the trees to the west. Almost immediately, pass another path on the left, which leads to fallen tree limbs and leaves, possibly filling in and covering a small sinkhole. Butterflies and birds, especially mourning doves, are numerous.

The trail squiggles a little to the right and left. In about 150 feet, another path heads to the left. Follow the path to reach Hide Out Sink. It is only 3 or 4 feet deep, but the rocks around it and the partially exposed limestone slab are noteworthy. The slab is a portion of the collapsed roof of the cave. Walking through the woods, with short paths leading to mysterious formations, can furnish opportunities for a great adventure for young children.

Reach a Y and follow the right branch a short distance to a bench and the fence around Goat Cave. Not much can be seen of Goat Cave due to the fence. The cave opening is about 25 feet in diameter. Continue north on the path as it gets a little rockier until it reaches the preserve boundary fence. Backtrack to the trailhead.

Miles and Directions

0.0   Start at the trailhead kiosk past the berm, at the north edge of Deer Lane. Head left, going north.

0.1   A narrow path on the left leads to Wade Sink, about 25 feet away. Return to the trail and follow it straight in a northeast direction.

0.2   Bear slightly left, still heading northeast, and pass a path on the left leading to Hide Out Sink. Return from the sinkhole and turn left onto the trail.

0.3   Reach a Y and take the right branch, still heading generally northeast. Bear slightly left and reach a wooden bench on the left and a fenced area protecting Goat Cave.

0.4   Return to the main trail and continue left (forward) until reaching the park boundary fence. Backtrack from here to the trailhead.

0.7   Arrive back at the trailhead and parking area.

9 Mary Moore Searight: Metro Loop Trail

This park has a number of intersecting trails, totaling over 6 miles, which makes it easy to alter the hike depending on the time available and amount of solitude wanted. These trails can be reached from the paved Metro Loop Trail. Spanish moss drapes many of the oak trees.

Distance: 2.4-mile lollipop
Approximate hiking time: 1.5 hours
Difficulty: Easy (due to flat terrain and paved trail)
Trail surface: Dirt, asphalt
Best season: Year-round
Other trail users: Joggers, dog walkers, equestrians
Canine compatibility: Leashed dogs permitted
Land status: Metro park; City of Austin Parks Department

Fees and permits: None
Schedule: 5:00 a.m. to 10:00 p.m.
Maps: No maps available in the park; visit the Web site www.ci .austin.tx.us/parks/traildirectory .htm for maps. USGS topo: Oak Hill, 7.5' quad
Trail contacts: Austin Parks and Recreation Department, 1600 City Park Rd., Austin 78730; (512) 346-3807 or (512) 974-6700

Finding the trailhead: From south Austin, take TX 71 west to I-35. Take I-35 south for 4 miles to the Slaughter Lane exit. Follow Slaughter Lane west 1.3 miles to the park entrance, at 407 Slaughter La. The Mary Moore Searight entrance road is just past Yarsa Boulevard. Proceed about 0.7 mile on the entrance road and park at the south side near the pavilion and restrooms. There are speed bumps on the entrance road—use caution. The asphalt trail is about 50 feet west from the parking area. *DeLorme: Texas Atlas & Gazetteer:* Page 69 G10. GPS: N30 09.759' / W97 48.473'

The Hike

At the pavilion and restrooms on the south side of the parking lot, head west on the sidewalk for about 50 feet to reach the asphalt trail. There are large boulders on the right and cedar trees on the left. Cross a wide dry section of creek bed that has a limestone bottom. This is a picturesque hike, great for dog walkers.

Go up a slight slope to a Y intersection in the trail and take the left branch. Follow the trail, bearing slightly to the right then left, and then pass a path on the left. Many of the live oaks are festooned with strands of Spanish moss. Watch for Spanish moss in some of the cedars, as this is unusual.

The graveled Equestrian Trail crosses the Metro Loop Trail three times, giving you the opportunity to shorten or lengthen the hike. Continue heading south to a T intersection and take the right branch to the west. The trail forms a counterclockwise loop from this point and completes the loop back at this intersection. There are some prickly pear cactus and low cedars on both sides of the trail.

A path on the right leads to a road and a subdivision. There are numerous exercise stations, including a set of monkey bars and chinning bars. The 380-acre park is becoming a refuge for local wildlife as residential construction around the park destroys their habitat. Early morning or late afternoon affords the best opportunity to see raccoon, opposum, deer, and, rarely, fox.

Several dirt paths cross the trail, and playing fields can be seen on the left. Pass under utility lines and follow along them for about 75 yards. Twelve large limestone blocks (3 feet high by 3 feet wide by 8 feet long) line the right side of

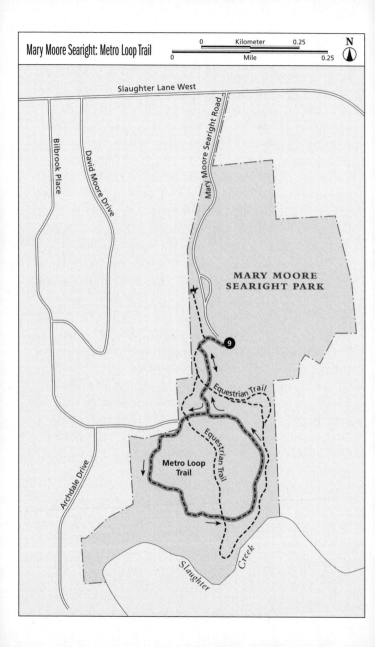

Mary Moore Searight: Metro Loop Trail

Kilometer

Mile

N

Slaughter Lane West

Bilbrook Place

David Moore Drive

Mary Moore Searight Road

MARY MOORE
SEARIGHT PARK

9

Equestrian Trail

Equestrian Trail

Archdale Drive

Metro Loop
Trail

Slaughter Creek

the trail. Some are low enough to sit on, providing a place to relax and enjoy the scenery.

Occasionally, traffic noise can be heard from Slaughter Lane to the north and I-35 to the east. This is a reminder that the hike is in the city.

Miles and Directions

0.0 Start at the trailhead adjacent to the main parking area, behind the restrooms, and head south.

0.1 Cross over a seasonally dry creek bed with a limestone bottom. Go up a slight slope to a Y intersection in the trail. Take the left branch, heading southeast.

0.3 Continue straight ahead. A path crosses the trail from the left.

0.5 Reach a T intersection and turn right, heading southwest. Pass an exercise station and bench on the right, shaded by large live oak trees.

0.7 Pass a large open area on the left that contains wildflowers. Residences are in view to the right. Follow the trail slightly uphill, and then make a hard left (south).

0.8 The trail bends right and left. Continue to follow the trail, passing a chinning bar on the right, and then bear left (southeast).

1.0 Pass by a dozen large (3 feet high by 3 feet wide by 8 feet long) rectangular limestone rocks on the right. Bear left (east) at the end of the large rocks.

1.3 Pass by a monkey bar exercise station on the right. The remains of an old barbed-wire fence go for a short distance to the right.

1.5 Pass an exercise station on the left. Follow the trail basically north, as it bends back and forth to the right and left.

1.8 Follow the trail as it loops to the left (northwest). There is a bench on the right, in the shade of a large live oak tree.

2.0 Reach a Y in the trail and take the right branch, heading north. The left branch goes back to the loop. This area should look familiar. Backtrack to the trailhead.

2.4 Arrive back at the trailhead.

10 Blunn Creek Preserve

Forty-acre Blunn Creek Nature Preserve, across the street from St. Edward's University, remains wild and natural. The trails are well marked and maintained, although portions are rocky and steep. Blunn Creek is forded twice while going from dense tree cover to hilly overlooks. A short out-and-back segment leads to the Volcano Overlook.

Distance: 1.5-mile counterclockwise loop

Approximate hiking time: 1 hour

Difficulty: Easy (due to length and shade)

Trail surface: Dirt with some rock (compressed volcanic ash)

Best season: Year-round

Other trail users: Bird-watchers

Canine compatibility: No dogs permitted

Land status: Nature preserve; City of Austin Parks Department

Fees and permits: None

Schedule: 5:00 a.m. to 10:00 p.m. daily

Maps: No maps available in the park; visit the Web site www.ci.austin.tx.us/parks/traildirectory.htm for maps. NCGS topo: Montopolis, 7.5' quad

Trail contacts: Austin Parks and Recreation Department, 1600 City Park Rd., Austin 78730; (512) 346-3807 or (512) 974-6700

Special considerations: No potable water or restroom facilities. No bikes allowed.

Finding the trailhead: From near downtown Austin, take Cesar Chavez Street to I-35. Enter I-35 and go south over the Colorado

River (Town Lake) for 2 miles, then take the Oltorf Street exit to the I-35 Frontage Road. Follow the Frontage Road south for 0.5 mile and turn right (west) onto St. Edwards Drive. Go about 3 blocks to 1200 St. Edwards Dr. The preserve is on the right (north) side of the road. Park along the curb. Since this is a public road, be sure to take any valuables with you and lock your car. *DeLorme: Texas Atlas & Gazetteer:* Page 93 K8. GPS: N30 13.556' / W97 44.518'

The Hike

Start at the West Creek Trail trailhead, on the north side of St. Edwards Drive. This hike combines portions of several trails in the preserve, and most parallel the creek. There are many branches and intersections, but they are well marked. The trail surface is mostly dirt, with some gravel and compressed volcanic rock. Some of the outcroppings and rocks were created by volcanoes that existed in Travis County about seventy million years ago.

Within 0.1 mile, take the trail on the right (east), which is the Creek Loop. Ford Blunn Creek, which is generally less than a foot deep. It is spring fed and flows year-round, furnishing good habitat for plants and wildlife. More than one hundred species of birds have been seen in the preserve. Add a dimension to the hike by watching for lark buntings, which sometimes cluster in flocks during the fall migration. This easy to identify, small, stocky, black bird has white patches on its wings and a large, bluish-gray beak.

Reach a T and turn left, heading north toward the Volcano Overlook. This is the hardest section of the hike, going over rock outcrops for about 60 feet, including a 30-foot increase in elevation. Large groups of prickly pear cactus, the state plant, reach to the trail's edge. At the top of the hill is the Volcano Overlook, a three-tiered section

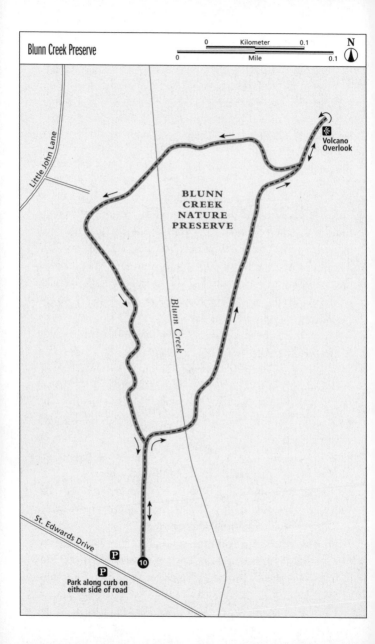

with interpretive signs and surrounded by rocks. The view, which includes St. Edward's University to the south and the creek bottomland, where hackberry, elms, and some persimmon trees thrive, is great. The main university building sits on top of the remains of a volcano. This is a good spot to just kick back and enjoy.

Backtrack from the overlook and turn west, crossing Blunn Creek. Watch for turtles sunning themselves on logs in the creek. Animal tracks can be seen along the creek edge, including those of armadillo, fox, and skunk. Mature live oak trees, some covered with Spanish moss, are in the woods. Get on the West Creek Trail heading southeast and cross the creek. This is an easy crossing since the creek bed is solid rock. Solid limestone outcrops line the west side of the creek. The water rushing over the many rocks creates a pleasant gurgling sound. Follow the trail south back to the trailhead.

Miles and Directions

0.0 Start at the West Creek Trail trailhead on the north side of St. Edwards Drive. Head directly north.

0.1 Reach a trail marker post on the right and a path intersecting from the right. Turn right, heading east, onto the Creek Loop Trail.

0.2 Reach a junction where the East Circle Trail joins from the right. Turn right (east) onto the East Circle Trail and cross Blunn Creek.

0.3 Reach a T and a trail marker post. Take the left branch, heading north on the East Branch Trail.

0.4 Bear slightly right and left, and then right, to reach a volcanic and limestone outcrop. Go up the outcrop for about 60 feet, with a 30-foot rise in elevation.

0.5 Reach a T and a trail marker post. Take the right branch, heading east to the Volcanic Overlook.

0.6 Reach the Volcanic Overlook, which has three levels. St. Edward's University can be seen to the southwest. Backtrack to the T and turn right, heading northwest.

0.8 Reach a Y with a very large (5-foot diameter) live oak tree. Take the left branch, heading west.

0.9 Follow the trail bearing left to reach Blunn Creek. The creek bed is solid flat limestone, making the crossing easy—except after a heavy rain. The trail heads up and is rough for about 40 feet.

1.0 Reach a Y and continue straight, and then bend left on the trail. The next section of the trail is rough, with limestone outcrops and pebbles across the trail.

1.2 A path intersects from the right. Continue to follow the trail straight (south).

1.3 Pass a trail marker post on the left, which points to the Creek Loop Trail. Continue to follow the trail straight, going south, and backtrack to the trailhead.

1.5 Arrive back at the trailhead.

11 St. Edwards Park: Hill and Creek Trails

St. Edwards Park offers a split personality—a high limestone bluff and flat lowlands separated by Bull Creek. Cross over slightly submerged rocks to the south side of Bull Creek and the Hill Trail. A steep section over limestone outcrops leads to the top, where a single-track trail clings to the edge of the bluff. There are impressive vistas of the countryside through clearings in the cedars.

Distance: 1.2-mile lollipop
Approximate hiking time: 1.5 hours
Difficulty: Moderate (due to steep inclines and declines over rocky terrain on the Hill Trail)
Trail surface: Dirt, stones, limestone outcrops
Best season: October to June
Other trail users: Dog walkers
Canine compatibility: Leashed dogs permitted. Dogs are not recommended on the Hill Trail due to the rocky terrain and the single-track trail on the edge of the bluff.
Land status: City park; Austin

Parks and Recreation Department
Fees and permits: None
Schedule: 5:00 a.m. to 10:00 p.m. daily
Maps: No maps available in the park; visit the Web site www.ci .austin.tx.us/parks/traildirectory .htm for maps. NCGS topo: Jollyville, 7.5' quad
Trail contacts: Austin Parks and Recreation Department, 1600 City Park Rd., Austin 78730; (512) 346-3807
Special considerations: No potable water or restroom facilities

Finding the trailhead: From US 183 in Austin, take the Capital of Texas Highway south to Spicewood Springs Road. Turn right (west) and go about 5 miles. Pass Bridge 5 and go 0.25 mile. The park entrance is on the left at 7301 Spicewood Springs Rd. There are two

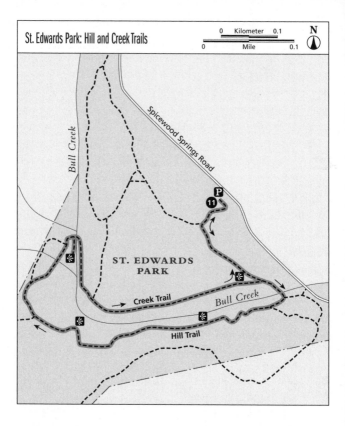

St. Edwards Park: Hill and Creek Trails

Kilometer

Mile

N

Bull Creek

Spicewood Springs Road

P

11

ST. EDWARDS
PARK

Creek Trail

Bull Creek

Hill Trail

trailhead posts. Start at the one to the left. *DeLorme: Texas Atlas & Gazetteer:* Page 92 A7. GPS: N30 24.390' / W97 47.413'

The Hike

Grassy areas with cedars and prickly pear cactus are interspersed on each side of the trail. Follow a gentle slope down, heading to Bull Creek. There is a narrow rock and concrete dam that some folks use to get across, but there is no trail to follow at the other side. The creek is shallow, so wading across presents no problem.

Once on the Hill Trail, climb about 50 feet up and over limestone outcroppings to where the trail levels. There are sections of single track that hug the edge of the bluff and have sheer drop-offs to the creek bed. This requires caution, since small rocks and tree roots are in the path. Bear left and go up some steep limestone "steps" that lead to a flat area near the top of the bluff. There are a few rocks that are large enough to sit on and take a rest after the climb. Several trails enter this area, but continue to the right, heading west along the edge of the bluff. Clearings between the cedar and oak trees allow panoramic views of the creek lowlands. At the top, the stillness, silence, and serenity make it difficult to believe this is in Austin. Take the path to the right and head slightly down to a boundary fence, where the trail makes a hard right. Getting to the top and getting down are the most strenuous parts of the hike. Go steeply downhill for about 75 feet over solid limestone outcrops, some requiring a step down of 3 feet. After a section of single track, the trail widens. The creek comes into view and is wide, with gravel, sandbars, and a few trees, making an ideal watering hole for deer. The path along the north side of the creek leads to and dead-ends at limestone bluffs bordering it. This out-and-back path is the only place in the park where the bluffs can be viewed. The path is narrow and overgrown, and it appears that not many folks get here. Backtrack to the point where you turned onto this path and cross the stream to the Creek Trail. Go past numerous branches, generally staying right. Continue to follow the trail back to the parking area. This park has a proliferation of unmarked paths. Fortunately, getting lost is not a major problem if you use the bluff, Bull

Creek, and Spicewood Springs Road as reference points. Although this hike is short, it is invigorating and scenic.

Miles and Directions

0.0 Start at the Creek Trail trailhead adjacent to the parking area. Creek Trail leads to a junction with the Hill Trail across Bull Creek.

0.1 After leaving the trailhead, quickly reach a Y. (It is actually less than 100 yards.) Take the left (southeast) leg and continue left past another branch. Many of these paths have been made by hikers and wander through the park.

0.2 Reach Bull Creek. Spicewood Springs Road can be seen about 50 yards to the left (east). Cross Bull Creek to the trailhead for the Hill Trail. Continue across a trail that passes on the left and right, and start up the hill. Limestone steps lead to a T. Take the right leg and head west, following Bull Creek.

0.3 Near the top of the bluff, there is a flat open area where three other trails enter. Continue right (west) along the edge of the bluff and overlooking the creek.

0.6 Reach the top of the bluff, which overlooks Bull Creek to the north. Other trails enter the area on the left, but continue bearing right, close to the edge of the bluff.

0.7 Reach Keith's Overlook (named for yours truly) for a clear view of Bull Creek plains. Start a steep descent to the creek.

0.8 After the descent, reach the east side of Bull Creek. Turn right on a path that heads south, and go about 30 yards to where it dead-ends at a limestone bluff. This is the only place where the bluffs can be reached. Backtrack to Hill Trail and ford Bull Creek to the Creek Trail.

0.9 Bear left (east) on the Creek Trail. Bull Creek is on the right.

1.1 Make a hard left (north) turn and backtrack to the trailhead.

1.2 Arrive back at the trailhead.

12 Barton Creek Greenbelt: Gus Fruh Access

The Gus Fruh Access to the Barton Creek Greenbelt provides great scenery and some difficult single-track hiking along Barton Creek. The greenbelt opened in 1985 and is the patriarch of all hiking trails within the city. These trails are best enjoyed if hiked in segments via one of the six access points.

Distance: 2.7-mile narrow clockwise loop

Approximate hiking time: 2 hours

Difficulty: More challenging (due to limestone outcrops and single track on lower trail)

Trail surface: Lower trail is dirt and limestone; upper trail is dirt and crushed gravel

Best season: Year-round

Other trail users: Dog walkers, mountain bikers

Canine compatibility: Leashed dogs permitted

Fees and permits: None

Schedule: 5:00 a.m. to 10:00 p.m. daily

Maps: No maps available in the park, but at the trailhead there is a kiosk with large trail map. You can also find maps on the Web site www.ci.austin.tx.us/parks/parkmaps. NCGS topo: Austin West, 7.5' quad

Trail contacts: Austin Parks and Recreation Department, 1600 City Park Rd., Austin 78730; (512) 346-3807 or (512) 974-6700

Special considerations: Trail may be closed after heavy rains. Call (512) 472-1267 for information. No potable water or restroom facilities.

Finding the trailhead: From near downtown Austin, take Cesar Chavez Street to Lamar Boulevard. Turn left and enter Lamar Boulevard and go south over the Colorado River. Continue on Lamar Boulevard for 2.4 miles and exit at the Barton Skyway. Follow Barton Skyway northwest for 0.75 mile and exit onto Barton Hills Drive.

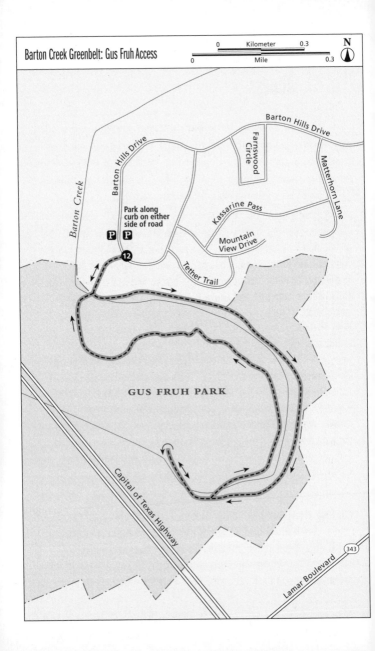

Barton Creek Greenbelt: Gus Fruh Access

Kilometer

Mile

N

Barton Hills Drive

Farnswood Circle

Barton Hills Drive

Matterhorn Lane

Barton Creek

Barton Hills Drive

Kassarine Pass

Park along curb on either side of road

Mountain View Drive

P P

12

Tether Trail

GUS FRUH PARK

Capital of Texas Highway

Lamar Boulevard

343

Follow Barton Hills Drive west for about 6 blocks to 2642 Barton Hills Dr. Park along the curb. The Gus Fruh entrance to the greenbelt and trailhead is on the south side of the road. Remember to take valuables with you and lock your vehicle, since this is a public road. *DeLorme: Texas Atlas & Gazetteer:* Page 93 H7. GPS: N30 14.968' / W97 47.711'

The Hike

Start at the Gus Fruh trailhead and head south. This hike is a favorite of mountain bikers and dog walkers. Nonvenomous and venomous snakes call the greenbelt home, but the dog walkers and mountain bikers discourage these critters. Take a map, or study the kiosk at the trailhead, which has a park map. Stay on the trail paralleling Barton Creek, since some of the paths created by the bikers can be confusing. The greenbelt contains 770 acres, and the adjoining Barton Creek Wilderness contains 1,000 acres, more than enough space to get seriously disoriented. Take water, a hat, and sunscreen. The greenbelt trails have been rated as the seventh-best hike in Texas.

The first section of the trail is crushed gravel and 6 feet wide. Follow it south along the creek, and within a short distance reach the Gus Fruh Pool. The pool is formed by springs and a wide area in the creek. During times of scant rainfall or drought (2007–2008), the pool may be dry, baring the rocks and limestone of the creek bed. Follow the trail east as it narrows to single track along sheer limestone cliffs. This section is difficult, with slight ups and downs over limestone outcrops. Ashe juniper, black willow, oak, and elm cover the terrain.

When the creek is flowing, there are numerous pools deep enough for swimming. In periods of little rain, the creek can be dry except for shallow pools and some springs; however, the dry creek bed gives the opportunity to add a little adventure to the hike and use it as the trail. The bed is about 35 feet wide, full of boulders, limestone slabs, and a few small pools to skirt around. The more difficult lower trail is on the north and east side of the creek, while the upper trail is on the south and west side, so crossing from one to the other is easy.

After about 1 mile there is a cliff overhang on the south side of the creek. Small springs seep through the limestone, creating a pool deep enough to wade or, sometimes, swim in. A short distance beyond these springs, cross the creek and pick up the upper trail. Follow the trail until reaching a GUS FRUH ACCESS sign. Cross the creek and backtrack to the trailhead.

Miles and Directions

0.0 Start at the Gus Fruh Access trailhead on the south side of 2642 Barton Hills Dr. and head south on the lower trail toward Barton Creek.

0.1 Continue to follow the trail, passing a branch from the right. Then bend left, heading east on single track along Barton Creek.

0.2 Pass the Gus Fruh Pool, formed by springs and the creek.

0.3 Tall limestone cliffs border the left edge of the trail. Walking is difficult on the limestone outcrops. There is a choice here, depending if Barton Creek is dry: 1) Continue on the single-track lower trail; 2) Cross the creek to upper trail; or 3) Walk down the dry creek bed. Both the upper trail (south and west side of creek) and lower trail (north and east side of creek) are adjacent to the creek. For easier walking and better views, walk down the dry creek bed.

0.5 Pass by an overhanging rock shelter created by the cliffs on the left.

0.9 The lower trail temporarily ends due to cliffs coming down to the creek edge.

1.0 Pass by small springs on the left (south) side of the creek. This is a favorite spot for hikers to cool off.

1.4 Barton Creek curves northwest and narrows, with dense growth on both sides. Backtrack, heading south for less than 0.1 mile. Cross the creek bed where it turns left, heading east, and get on the upper trail. Continue to follow the trail until it bends left and heads north, still bordering the creek.

1.7 Pass three paths on the right that lead to the creek, which is about 70 feet away.

2.0 Reach a T and take the right branch, heading north. Then bear left, heading west, staying close to the creek.

2.3 Reach a T and take the right branch, heading north.

2.4 Reach a Gus Fruh Access sign on the right that points to the right and the creek. Cross the creek and backtrack to the trailhead on the lower trail.

2.7 Arrive back at the trailhead.

13 Barton Creek Greenbelt: Gaines Creek Access

The hike to Twin Falls and Sculpture Falls is a magnet for nature lovers, dog walkers, waders, and mountain bikers. The trail follows Barton Creek, which splits the greenbelt and is bordered by sheer cliff walls. The creek may be dry, depending on the rainfall. Vegetation is thick, lush, and varied. This is the most popular hike in Austin.

Distance: 3.2 miles out and back

Approximate hiking time: 2.5 hours

Difficulty: Moderate (due to some single-track rocky sections)

Trail surface: Dirt and rock

Best season: Year-round

Other trail users: Dog walkers, mountain bikers, joggers

Canine compatibility: Leashed dogs permitted

Land status: City park; City of Austin Parks Department

Fees and permits: None

Schedule: 5:00 a.m. to 10:00 p.m. daily

Maps: No maps available in the park, but at the trailhead there is a kiosk with large trail map. Also, visit the Web site www.ci.austin .tx.us/parks/traildirectory.htm for maps. NCGS topo: Oak Hill, 7.5' quad

Trail contacts: Austin Parks and Recreation Department, 1600 City Park Rd., Austin 78730; (512) 346-3807 or (512) 974-6700

Special considerations: Some trails may be closed after a heavy rain; call the Barton Creek hotline at (512) 472-1267. No potable water or restroom facilities available on the trail.

Finding the trailhead: From the MoPac Expressway southbound, take the Loop 360 exit (Capital of Texas Highway). Head south on the MoPac access road. Go past the freeway entrance, and the trailhead is on the right. The Gaines Creek Access is at 3900 South

The Hike

Check the kiosk at the trailhead to become familiar with the trails. Head right (north) along the canyon rim and then down. Dog walkers, mountain bikers, and folks eager to go wading share the trail. Stay to the right and be alert to speeding bikers. Take water, a hat, and sunscreen.

The dirt trail is narrow and winds its way through heavy woods of oaks and cedars. Much of the trail is flat, but some climbing and careful footwork are necessary. Along Barton Creek, the variety of trees expands to include ash, birch, black willow, elm, pecan, sycamore, and sugarberry. The creek is named for William "Uncle Billy" Barton, who settled in the area in 1837 near what was called Spring Creek but is now known as Barton Creek.

Reach Twin Falls, the high point of the hike. A wide limestone shelf that drops down about 6 feet creates the falls. Texans, in their longing for waterfalls and mountains, have special definitions for what qualifies: A waterfall is any creek or river that drops 4 feet or more, and a mountain is any hill over 4,000 feet. When the creek is flowing, Twin Falls is a favorite location for waders and swimmers.

Overhangs, caves, and nooks and crannies can be seen on the face of the cliffs. Local legend claims that Robert E. Lee made numerous trips here and that notorious criminals Bonnie and Clyde, Jesse James, and Sam Bass used the small caves as hideouts. Some hikers report that when the creek is dry, wagon ruts can be seen in the limestone bed. The tracks were worn into the limestone when the creek bed was used as a route into town.

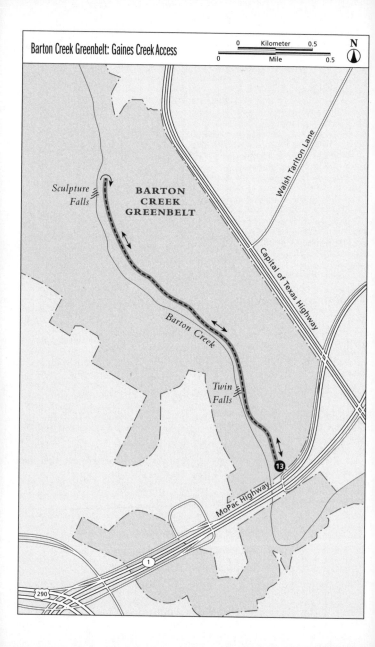

Barton Creek Greenbelt: Gaines Creek Access

Kilometer

Mile

N

Sculpture
Falls

BARTON
CREEK
GREENBELT

Walsh Tarlton Lane

Capital of Texas Highway

Barton Creek

Twin
Falls

13

MoPac Highway

1

290

When the creek is flowing, it is relatively shallow, but it is deep enough to support tubers, kayakers, and lots of good swimming holes. The dry creek can add a bit of adventure if it is used as part of the trail. Skirting around large exposed sun-bleached boulders and limestone outcrops sometimes requires skills not needed on the official trail. Watch for venomous and nonvenomous snakes near the creek, although the mountain bikers and dog walkers really discourage them. Stay near the creek while hiking and avoid taking paths made by adventurous hikers and bikers. This can lead to disorientation.

Continue to follow the trail north to Sculpture Falls. The strange-looking rock formations carved by the creek provide many photo ops. There are rapids around the falls that, along with the towering cliffs, add to the ambience. The rock ledges there are a good place to sit, have a snack, and enjoy the scenery. Backtrack to the trailhead.

Miles and Directions

- **0.0** Start at the Gaines Creek Access. Check the map at the kiosk at the trailhead for orientation. Head right (north) along the canyon rim.
- **0.1** Reach the canyon floor and continue north.
- **0.2** Pass a marker post and continue on the upper trail.
- **0.3** Reach Twin Falls on the left. Continue heading north on the upper trail.
- **0.7** Follow the trail left, heading northwest.
- **1.2** Bear left, heading north. Pass many paths leading to the creek and the woods.
- **1.6** Reach Sculpture Falls. It is possible to cross the creek near the falls. Backtrack to the trailhead.
- **3.2** Arrive back at the trailhead.

14 Wild Basin Wilderness Preserve

This is one of Austin's most pristine nature preserves. The trails wind through granite outcrops, woods, and grasslands and near Bee Creek. A small waterfall about halfway through the hike is refreshing. It's home to the black-capped vireo, a threatened species, and hundreds of other bird species. There are many interpretive stations along the trail, making it a great hike for nature lovers.

Distance: 2.1-mile counterclockwise loop of interconnecting short trails

Approximate hiking time: 2 hours (to allow time to read interpretive information)

Difficulty: Moderate (due to limestone outcrops and minor elevation changes)

Trail surface: Dirt, limestone

Best season: Year-round

Other trail users: Bird-watchers, student study groups

Canine compatibility: Dogs not allowed

Land status: Nature preserve; City of Austin Parks Department

Fees and permits: Voluntary day-use fee based on the honor system. (Be honorable.)

Schedule: Sunrise to sunset daily

Maps: Interpretive trail maps are available at the Environmental Education Center and at a kiosk at the trailhead. Maps are also available at the Web site www .wildbasin.org. USGS topo: Austin West, 7.5' quad

Trail contacts: Austin Parks and Recreation Department, 1600 City Park Rd., Austin 78730; (512) 346-3807 or (512) 327-7622

Special considerations: Bicycles not allowed. Picnicking not allowed. No potable water or restroom facilities on the trail. Portable toilets near the parking area. Guided tours are available.

Finding the trailhead: From near downtown Austin, take the First Street entrance onto the MoPac Expressway. Head south on MoPac for 3 miles to the Capital of Texas Highway exit. Exit onto Capital of Texas Highway and head north for 5 miles to 805 North Capital of Texas Hwy. Turn right into the entrance of Wild Basin and check in at the environmental education center. *DeLorme: Texas Atlas & Gazetteer:* Page 92 F5. GPS: N30 18.370' / W97 49.151'

The Hike

Start at the trailhead behind the environmental education center, heading east and then south. The center has a great deck that overlooks the valley. Seven short trails (Arroyo Loop, Laurel, Falls, Creek, Woodland, Ledge, and Triknee) are combined in this hike to form a counterclockwise loop. The trails are bordered on the west side by Northwest Hollow, which empties into Bee Creek. Sections of the preserve are close to Highway 360, so vehicle noise can be heard.

Be sure to pick up an interpretive trail map at the environmental education center. There are forty-six interpretive stations spaced along the trails that describe the flora and fauna, so be prepared to spend extra time on the hike. All the trail branches and intersections are well marked. The entire preserve is environmentally sensitive, so it's important to stay on marked trails. The trails in the first half of the hike head gently down, while those in the last half have an elevation increase of more than 300 feet. The canopy cover alternates between dense shade and open sky. Bring a hat, water, and sunscreen.

About a half mile into the hike, reach interpretive station 9, where mountain laurel shrubs are shown and described. They are the harbingers of spring with their showy clusters of bluish purple flowers, and in the fall their seeds are hard

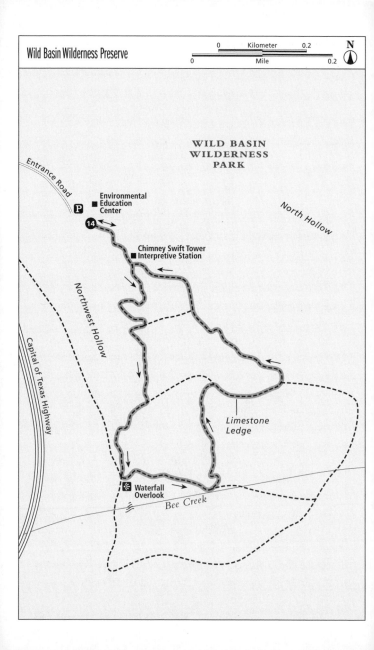

0   Kilometer   0.2

0   Mile   0.2

N

WILD BASIN
WILDERNESS
PARK

Entrance Road

North Hollow

Environmental
Education Center

P

14

Chimney Swift Tower
Interpretive Station

Northwest Hollow

Capital of Texas Highway

Limestone
Ledge

Waterfall
Overlook

Bee Creek

shelled and red. The flowers and seeds are very poisonous if eaten by humans or animals, so alert your curious young folks.

Continue heading south on the Arroyo Loop Trail until you reach the intersection with the Laurel Trail. Take the Laurel Trail south until it ends at the Falls Trail. Follow the Falls Trail south to the small waterfall on Bee Creek. There is a concrete bench in a shaded area that overlooks the falls and creek. This is a good spot for photo ops. Take the Creek Trail east, passing interpretive markers G through K, and then turn left (north) at the Woodland Trail.

The Woodland Trail has a steep section where water bars and limestone outcrops act as steps. It can be strenuous going up and down these steps. There are sharp 15- to 20-foot drop-offs on the left side. Turn right onto the Ledge Trail, heading east. About 20 feet from the trail there is a low limestone outcrop that gave the Ledge Trail its name. Follow the Ledge to the junction of Possum and Triknee. On Triknee there is a wood bench with board slats over the top to shield the sun. Take Triknee to Arroyo, and then backtrack.

Miles and Directions

0.0 Start at the Arroyo Vista trailhead behind the environmental education center. Pay the voluntary entrance fee at the donation box. Follow the trail a short way east, and then head south.

0.1 Pass the Arroyo Vista and Waterfall, 0.7 mile trail marker on the left.

0.2 Pass the Chimney Swift Tower interpretive station on the left. Reach a Y and take the right branch (south), and then bend right (west).

0.3 Reach interpretive stations 5 and 6, and make a hard left, heading south.

0.4 Take a hard left, making a semicircle to the right and heading west.

0.5 Heading southeast, reach a trail intersection with the Laurel Trail and a waterfall on the right. Turn right, heading south, and pass interpretive sign 10. The trail surface is rough and rocky.

0.6 Reach a T and take the right branch, bearing southwest toward the waterfall. The left branch goes to the Ledge Trail.

0.8 Reach the overlook for the waterfall on Bee Creek. At the overlook, turn left (east) onto the Creek Trail. The Madrone Trail is to the right.

1.0 The Woodland Trail intersects from the left. Turn left onto the Woodland Trail and head north toward the Ledge Trail.

1.3 The Woodland Trail Ts into the Ledge Trail. Turn right onto the Ledge Trail, heading east toward the Possum Trail.

1.5 After bearing left and heading north, intersect the Possum and Triknee Trails. Turn left onto the Triknee Trail, heading northwest.

1.7 Follow the Triknee Trail to where it ends and joins the Arroyo Vista Trail. Continue straight on the Arroyo Vista for a short distance west, and then make a hard right, heading north.

1.9 Bear left, heading west; cross a short bridge; and continue to follow the Arroyo Vista to interpretive station 2. Backtrack from this point to the trailhead and the environmental education center.

2.1 Arrive back at the trailhead.

15 Emma Long Metropolitan Park: Turkey Creek Trail

Turkey Creek is the hike for creek lovers and dog lovers. Dogs who love to splash in the water get ample opportunity, as the creek is crossed no fewer than fourteen times. A variety of vegetation, including cedar, cedar elm, live oak, and mountain laurel, lines the creek bed. Follow a modest ascent from the creek, leaving the valley, to the top of the bluff, and break into the open sky at the canyon rim.

Distance: 2.6-mile lollipop
Approximate hiking time: 1.5 hours
Difficulty: Moderate (due to some rocky terrain and a 250-foot elevation gain up a steep hill)
Trail surface: Dirt path
Best season: Year-round
Other trail users: Dog walkers
Canine compatibility: Dogs permitted (leashes not required)
Land status: City park; Austin Parks and Recreation Department
Fees and permits: None

Schedule: 7:00 a.m. to 10:00 p.m. daily
Maps: Maps are available at the park office and on the Web site www.ci.austin.tx.us/parks/park directory.htm. NCGS topo: Austin West, 7.5' quad
Trail contacts: Austin Parks and Recreation Department, 1600 City Park Rd., Austin 78730; (512) 346-3807 or (512) 974-6700
Special considerations: No potable water or restroom facilities at the trailhead

Finding the trailhead: From central Austin, take Farm Road 2222 west, past Loop 360. Turn left onto City Park Road and continue south to the Emma Long park entrance sign. The parking area for the trail is on the right side of the road, 2 miles from the entrance. The

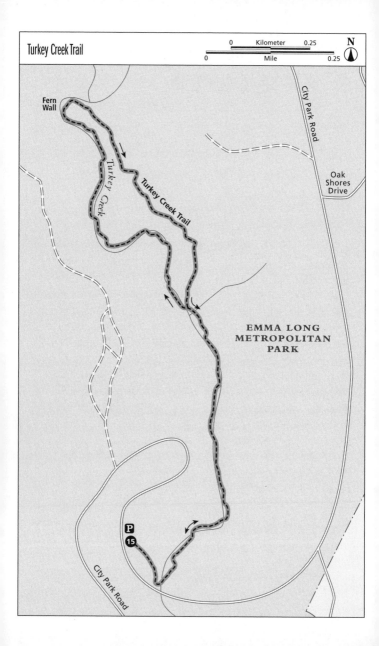

sign in the parking lot identifies the trail as a nature trail. The trail-head is adjacent to the parking lot and has a signboard with a map and trail information. *DeLorme: Texas Atlas & Gazetteer:* Page 93 C5. GPS: N30 20.008' / W97 50.400'

The Hike

This is one of only a few trails in the Austin area that allow dogs to be off-leash. The upside is that the dogs, and some-times their owners, enjoy uninhibited splashing in the creek; the downside is that the opportunity to see wildlife, other than birds, is rare.

As you get under way, follow the trail for a short distance parallel to City Park Road, and then cross over concrete stepping stones to the west side of Turkey Creek. This is the first of many creek crossings. Cedar trees furnish good cover and provide a cooling effect. After the first creek crossing, the trail heads generally north toward the Fern Wall. There is a large flat limestone outcrop in the creek bed just after the branch that begins the loop, which makes crossing the creek easier. At the fork, take the left branch; this keeps the mile markers in sequence. The trail closely follows the creek for about 1.25 miles, until you reach the Fern Wall. This wall, 40 to 50 feet high and alive with maidenhair ferns in the spring, is one of the limestone bluffs that border parts of the creek. After passing the Fern Wall, the trail heads south. Along the creek bank the cedars are joined by a few live oak, tall cedar elm, and sycamore trees. There have been ten creek crossings by the time the 1.5 mile marker is reached. The trail ascends about 250 feet and wanders away from Turkey Creek. The path is steep, with rocks and outcrops of limestone forming steps. The top is reached near the 1.5 mile marker, where the terrain flattens and becomes more open. Several paths lead to overlooks where great views of the creek and valley can be seen. Be careful when approaching the edge of the bluff since there are 40- to 50-foot drop-offs. On the way down from the summit there are more limestone steps, some dropping 5 feet down to the next step. Coming up the hill to the top and starting the descent down are the most strenuous parts of the hike. Going down, the path squirms through stands of cedars and reaches the creek. When the branch connecting the loop is reached, backtrack to the trailhead. Emma Long Metropolitan Park is one of many parks that the Civilian Conservation Corps (CCC) helped build. The CCC was established by President Franklin D. Roosevelt. Emma Long Metropolitan Park was originally known as City Park, and in 1984 it was renamed to honor Emma Long, the first woman to serve on the Austin City Council.

Miles and Directions

0.0 Start at the Turkey Creek trailhead adjacent to the parking area. Trail markers are placed at quarter-mile intervals.

0.75 Reach the branch that begins the loop. Take the left leg, along the creek edge, to walk the loop clockwise. This also keeps the mile markers in sequence.

1.0 Reach a mile marker. Turkey Creek will have been crossed eight times at this point.

1.5 A path near the top of the bluff leads to an overlook of the creek and valley.

2.0 Reach the branch connecting the loop. Continue south on the trail and backtrack to the trailhead.

2.6 Arrive back at the trailhead.

16 Commons Ford: Lake Austin Loop

This 215-acre underutilized park is great for families and beginning hikers. The short trail follows a robust creek, a line of towering pecan trees, and cliffs along the shores of Lake Austin, which is actually the Colorado River. Watch for turtles in the creek. The water and vegetation also furnish good habitat for birds; more than 120 species have been sighted in the park.

Distance: 1.6-mile counterclockwise loop

Approximate hiking time: 0.75 hour

Difficulty: Easy due to dirt trail and little elevation

Trail surface: Dirt, grass

Best season: Year-round

Other trail users: Dog walkers, bird-watchers

Canine compatibility: Leashed dogs permitted

Land status: Metro park; City of Austin Parks Department

Fees and permits: None

Schedule: 1:00 p.m. to 6:00 p.m. Tuesday through Sunday; automatic gate

Maps: No maps available in the park, but there is a kiosk near the rental cabin with a park map. Visit the Web site www.ci.austin.tx.us/parks/traildirectory.htm for maps. NCGS topo: Bee Cave, 7.5' quad

Trail contacts: Austin Parks and Recreation Department, 1600 City Park Rd., Austin 78730; (512) 346-3807 or (512) 974-6700

Finding the trailhead: From northwest Austin, follow TX 71 west to FM 2244. Turn right and head east on FM 2244 and go 4.6 miles to Commons Ford Park Road. After 0.6 mile pass Cuernavaca Drive on the right. Continue on Commons Ford Road for 1.6 miles to the park entrance gate. Turn left onto the park road and park near the creek. The trailhead is on the north side of the park road. *DeLorme: Texas Atlas & Gazetteer:* Page 92 F10. GPS: N30 20.173' / W97 53.147'

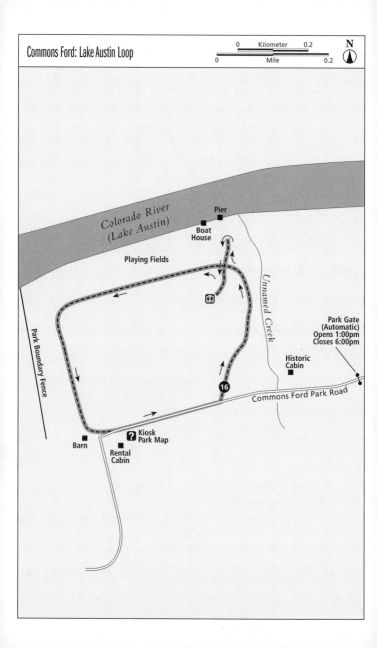

Commons Ford: Lake Austin Loop

0 Kilometer 0.2
0 Mile 0.2

N

Colorado River
(Lake Austin)

Pier

Boat House

Playing Fields

Unnamed Creek

Park Gate
(Automatic)
Opens 1:00pm
Closes 6:00pm

Historic Cabin

16

Park Boundary Fence

Commons Ford Park Road

Barn

Kiosk
Park Map

Rental Cabin

The Hike

Start this hike, also known as the Pecan Grove Loop, on the north side of the park road and follow an unnamed creek on the right (east) that heads north and empties into Lake Austin. The area around the trailhead is notable due to the large number of mature live oak trees that adjoin it. Remnants of a fence can be seen east of the creek. Very large live oaks, interspersed with a few sycamores, are scattered on both sides of the trail. Many of the live oaks have Spanish moss trailing from them.

Dog walkers and bird-watchers enjoy this park. The park grounds are mowed, with scattered trees and practically no shrubs. At the top of the hill, the terrain flattens. There is a brick fireplace, two picnic tables, and a fire grill on the left (west) side of the trail.

The creek widens as it bends northwest toward Lake Austin. It's worth going the short distance to the creek's edge to look for turtles and fish. In spring, groups of tadpoles can be seen swimming in pools next to the creek. Watch and listen for the more than 120 species of birds that make their home in the park. Seventeen types of sparrows—small birds that feed on the ground and often are unafraid of people—have been sighted.

Continue north toward Lake Austin. Pass by a small picnic area and playing fields used for badminton, volleyball, and Frisbee. There is a boathouse and dock on the shore of the lake (actually, the Colorado River), and small motorboats usually cruise the area. Backtrack south to the line of large pecan trees, for which the trail is named. The small building at the top of the hill is the restroom facility. Turn right and head west, following what appears to be a jeep path. Lake

Austin is on the right, and cliffs can be seen above its north shore. The next 0.8 mile has no shade, so if hiking in the summer, be sure to have a hat, water, and sunscreen.

Follow the trail south through a meadow and reach the park road. At this point there is a barn, a rental cabin, and a kiosk with a map of the park. Turn left, heading east, and follow the park road back to the trailhead.

Miles and Directions

0.0 Start at the trailhead just past the creek and on the north side of the entrance road and head north.

0.1 Follow trail north and head up a hill. A creek is on the right.

0.2 Pass a wooden vehicle bridge on the right (east) that crosses the creek.

0.3 Continue north and pass a large brick fireplace on the left with two picnic tables and a grill.

0.4 Reach the edge of Lake Austin (Colorado River). There is a boathouse and pier.

0.5 Backtrack to the line of large pecan trees and turn right (west). Turn left, shortly heading south toward the restroom facility. Investigate the restrooms and backtrack to the edge of the pecan trees, then turn left, heading west.

1.0 Follow the jeep path west and turn left (south) at the top of the hill.

1.3 Follow the trail south until the park entrance road. A barn is ahead, and the park rental cabin is across the road. There is a kiosk there with a park map. Turn left, heading east to the trailhead.

1.6 Arrive back at the trailhead.

17 Walnut Creek Metro

This park offers a large number of crisscrossing trails. This can add a dimension to the hike for those seeking variety. Cross Tar Branch Creek and Walnut Creek. Wildlife is abundant, but it can be difficult to see due to mountain bikers and dog walkers. Both venomous and nonvenomous snakes may be near the creeks.

Distance: 2.2-mile loop with some out and back
Approximate hiking time: 1.5 hours
Difficulty: Moderate (due to some steep portions of the trail)
Trail surface: Gravel, dirt
Best season: Year-round
Other trail users: Dog walkers, joggers, mountain bikers
Canine compatibility: Leashed dogs permitted
Land status: Metro park; City of
Austin Parks Department
Fees and permits: None
Schedule: 5:00 a.m. to 10:00 p.m. daily
Maps: No maps available in the park; visit the Web site www.ci .austin.tx.us/parks/trail directory.htm for maps. NCGS topo: Pflugerville West, 7.5' quad
Trail contacts: Austin Parks and Recreation Department, 1600 City Park Rd., Austin 78730; (512) 346-3807 or (512) 974-6700

Finding the trailhead: From north Austin, at the junction of US 183 and North Lamar Boulevard, turn right (north) onto North Lamar. Continue heading north, and in 2.7 miles pass Braker Lane. Stay on North Lamar Boulevard for 1.1 miles, and then turn left (west) onto Walnut Creek Park Road. Park in the lot near the swimming pool. The trailhead is to the south of the pool. *DeLorme: Texas Atlas & Gazetteer:* Page 93 B10. GPS: N30 24.026' / W97 41.035'

The Hike

Start the hike at the trailhead, which is a T branch. The park

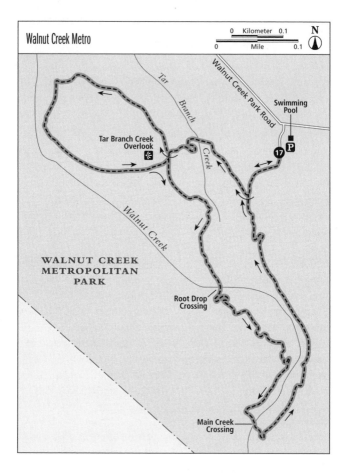

Walnut Creek Metro

0 Kilometer 0.1
0 Mile 0.1
N

Tar Branch

Creek

Walnut Creek Park Road

Swimming Pool

Tar Branch Creek Overlook

17
P

Walnut Creek

WALNUT CREEK
METROPOLITAN
PARK

Root Drop
Crossing

Main Creek
Crossing

offers a maze of trails, which can be confusing at times. Fortunately, the trails are well marked with signposts that include a number assigned by the park to identify their location. Mountain bikers use the park extensively, so keep to the right. There are several off-leash areas where dogs can frolic in the creek. An electrical substation adjoins the park and has three transmission lines that obtrusively cross over the trails.

Follow the trail into heavy cedar woods where the trees form an arch that blocks the sun. Cross Tar Branch Creek heading west and then north. The path leading to it has been deeply eroded by bikers. After crossing the creek, reach the Tar Branch Trail. The canopy cover varies from good shade to open. A hat, water, and sunscreen are suggested. This section of the trail slopes down and heads generally northwest, and then makes a hard left turn heading southeast toward Tar Branch Creek. At times the trail becomes single track, little more than a bike rut. Low-growing prickly pear cactus, the state plant, flourish in open space between the trees. Follow the ridge along the creek, but use caution because there are sheer drop-offs of 20 feet.

Follow the trail as it loops east and then bends south. Walnut Creek can be seen ahead, and also a creek crossing known as "Root Drop." The path down to the crossing is very steep, and after a rain it can be nearly impossible to navigate. This is the most difficult of the three creek crossings. Portions of the opposite shore (south) are solid limestone. The shallow water, usually less than 12 inches deep, rushes over a series of rocks, creating a pleasant gurgling sound. Look into the clear water for minnows and turtles. This is a very scenic area.

Continue on the trail in an east-to-west semicircle and reach the main crossing of Walnut Creek, identified by a MAIN CREEK CROSSING sign. Cross the creek, which is about 50 feet wide and has a limestone bed. Sometimes it's possible to hear the barking of dogs as they romp in the water. The creek is close by on the left, with numerous paths leading to overlooks. Follow the trail north past meadows and mixed hardwoods and cedars. Reach a bench in a shaded area that overlooks the creek, and then backtrack to the trailhead.

Miles and Directions

Note: The "location" number is the designation Walnut Creek Park has assigned to that marker.

0.0   Start at the trailhead just south of the parking lot by the swimming pool. The trailhead is a T; take the right branch, heading west.

0.2   Reach a Y (location 258) and take the left branch. Cross Tar Branch Creek.

0.3   Intersect with the Tar Branch Trail and turn right, heading north.

0.5   Reach a T (location 316) and take the left branch, heading south. Walk under power lines.

0.7   Reach a T and take the left branch, heading southeast, and then curve east. Walnut Creek is on the right, to the west.

0.9   Reach a T and take the right branch, heading south on the Tar Branch Trail.

1.1   A path comes in from the right, identified as "Root Drop" (location 304)—a difficult creek crossing. Turn right and cross Walnut Creek.

1.3   Reach a Y (location 410) and take the left branch, heading east for a short distance, and then south.

1.6   Reach a Y (location 404) and take the left branch, heading south. Cross the creek at the Main Creek Crossing sign. The creek is about 50 feet wide.

1.7   Reach a trail marker (location 232)—continue straight, heading north.

1.9   Pass a path on the left (location 250), which leads to the Tar Branch Creek overlook.

2.0   Reach a Y (location 244). Take the right branch, which bears slightly right, still heading north. Then backtrack toward the trailhead.

2.2   Arrive back at the trailhead.

18 Berry Springs Park: Muy Grande

This is the only hike in Texas that loops through more than 1,100 pecan trees. It's also the best trail for beginners, families with small children, and persons needing wheelchair access. Follow along Berry Creek to the Mill Pond, where beavers live. There are six interconnecting loops in Berry Springs Park that create 5 miles of trails.

Distance: 1.3 miles of interconnecting loops
Approximate hiking time: 1 hour
Difficulty: Easy (due to the flatness and surface of the trail)
Trail surface: Concrete, packed gravel
Best season: Year-round
Other trail users: Dog walkers
Canine compatibility: Leashed dogs permitted
Land status: Williamson County park; Williamson County Parks & Recreation Department
Fees and permits: None
Schedule: 7:00 a.m. to 10:00 p.m. daily
Maps: The trail map is on the bulletin board at the trailhead. You can also get a map at the Web site www.wilco.org. NCGS topo: Georgetown, 7.5' quad
Trail contacts: Williamson County Park Office, 1801 CR 152, Georgetown 78626; (512) 260-4283

Finding the trailhead: From Austin, take I-35 north to the Williams Drive exit in Georgetown. Head east, turn left on North Austin Avenue, and then turn right onto Farm Road 971. Turn left onto CR 152 and continue past the hard right turn in the road. Cross Berry Creek; the park entrance is on the left. The park entrance sign, built from stone, is in the shape of a limestone kiln. Continue into the parking lot. The trailhead adjoins the parking lot. *DeLorme: Texas Atlas & Gazetteer:* Page 69 C11. GPS: N30 41.057' / W97 38.713'

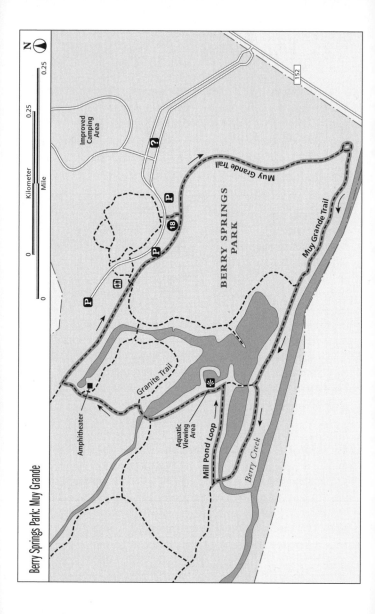

Berry Springs Park: Muy Grande

The Hike

Start the Muy Grande Loop, a concrete, wheelchair-accessible trail, by taking the left branch. More than 1,100 pecan trees, the state tree, come into view. The most striking thing is that the trees, planted in the mid-1920s, are in perfect rows exactly the same distance apart.

Follow the path to a walk-around circle. Circle to the right: Berry Creek is on the left about 30 yards down, and the dam crossing the creek at CR 152 is in sight. The dam, more than 160 years old, and the first grist mill in Williamson County, which operated near this site, were built by John Berry, a pioneer, colonist, gunsmith, blacksmith, and veteran of the War of 1812. (His great-grandson, Audie Murphy, was a World War II hero and the most decorated soldier in U.S. history.) Continue straight ahead; if you're hiking in July or August, the small white flowers of the obedience plant are noticeable along the creek. Go past a gravel path on the right; this is the Mill Pond Loop. Keep going to a boardwalk, actually concrete, which follows the creek for about 350 feet. Midway down the boardwalk on the right side is a 10-foot-high limestone dam that was built in 1846.

In spring and summer, the raucous cry of "ka, ka, ka, ka, ka, kowp, kowp, kowp, kowp" heard from the treetops can be startling. It is the call of the yellow-billed cuckoo, a medium-size bird with an appetite for tent caterpillars. Follow the path to a concrete bridge that crosses over the two-and-a-half-acre spring-fed Mill Pond. The spring water is a constant 68°F. Continue to follow the path in a northerly direction until the trail comes to a T at the junction with the Pond Loop Trail. Turn right; there is a bench on the left, and the pond is on the right. This is about the center of the park, and most of the 5 miles of trails are in your line of sight, so any route can be selected. Travel along the trail past a spur that goes to the amphitheater, and then turn right onto the concrete trail. Proceed along a narrow overflow section of Mill Pond. The Historic Compound, consisting of a 1920s-era house, a barn, and a small granary, is just past the shelter. The trailhead and parking lot are in view. Small children can easily go on this family-friendly hike and afterwards enjoy the catch-and-release fishing pond.

Miles and Directions

0.0 Start at the Muy Grande trailhead adjacent to the parking area and head left (east).

0.1 Pass a picnic bench on the left. Bear slightly left (east) and then right (south).

0.4 Reach the circle and bear right (west). Berry Creek is on the left (south). Reach the concrete boardwalk.

0.7 The boardwalk ends, and the Muy Grande Trail turns to hard-packed gravel. Reach a small concrete bridge crossing the pond overflow.

0.8 Reach a T intersection and follow the trail right (east). The pond is on the right.

0.9 Reach another T intersection and turn left (north) toward the amphitheater and the Muy Grande Trail.

1.0 Pass a path on the right (east) that leads to the amphitheater. Benches are placed near the trail.

1.1 Reach a T intersection with the Muy Grande. Turn right (east) and continue on Muy Grande.

1.3 Arrive back at the parking lot and trailhead.

19 Balcones Canyonlands National Wildlife Refuge: Cactus Rocks Trail

Texas Hill Country lovers and bird-watchers can combine the Cactus Rocks, Vista Knoll, and Ridgeline Trails to explore the Balcones limestone terraces in the Warbler Vista area of Balcones Canyonlands National Wildlife Refuge. Follow the Vista Knoll Trail down the backbone of a ridge and then back up for panoramic views of the Hill Country and Lake Travis. On the Cactus Rocks Trail, cactus appear to grow out of rocks.

Distance: 3.6 miles out and back

Approximate hiking time: 2.5 hours

Difficulty: Moderate (due to narrow trails on the edge of a bluff, with ups and downs on rocky trail)

Trail surface: Dirt, gravel, limestone outcrop

Best season: September to June

Other trail users: Bird-watchers April to June

Canine compatibility: Dogs not permitted

Land status: National wildlife refuge; U.S. Fish and Wildlife Service

Fees and permits: None

Schedule: Sunrise to sunset daily

Maps: Ask at the refuge office or visit the Web site http://friends ofbalcones.org/documents/ WV.pdf. NCGS topo: Nameless.

Trail contacts: Balcones Canyonlands National Wildlife Refuge, 24518 Farm Road 1431, Box 1, Marble Falls 78654; (512) 339-9432; www .fws.gov/southwest/refuges/ texas/balcones

Special considerations: No potable water is available. The only restroom is a portable toilet by the parking lot for the Cactus Rocks Trail.

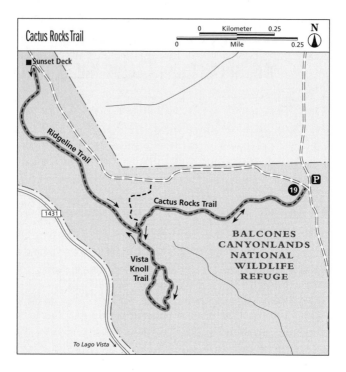

Finding the trailhead: The refuge is thirty minutes from Austin. From Austin, head north on US 183 to Cedar Park, about 14 miles. Turn left (west) onto FM 1431 and continue through Jamestown and Lago Vista. Turn right onto Farm Road 1174 and head north for about 5 miles. On the west side of Lago Vista look for the BALCONES CANYONLANDS NATIONAL WILDLIFE REFUGE sign on the right, and turn onto the gravel road. Drive downhill on the gravel road 0.75 mile to the Cactus Rocks parking area, next to the interpretive trail guide display. The trailhead is south of the park road and across from the parking lot. *DeLorme: Texas Atlas & Gazetteer:* Page 69 E9. GPS: N30 30.335' / W97 58.784'

The Hike

Pick up an interpretive trail brochure at the bulletin board located at the trailhead. Follow the trail into the cedar woods to interpretive marker 1, about 100 feet down the trail. These markers are unique in that they are made from limestone, with the face flattened and painted with the marker number and a picture of the golden-cheeked warbler. The more than 80,000 acres in the preserve were set aside to maintain habitat for the endangered warbler, which nests only in central Texas.

Head west and follow the contour of the ridge, where the limestone rimrock outcrops can be seen. Go down and up the sides of some dry gullies and pass prickly pear cactus growing from boulders and limestone outcroppings. The trail was named for the cactus that grow from the scant soil collected in the cracks and depressions in the rocks. Another interesting feature of the rocks is their "Swiss cheese" appearance—some of them are riddled with holes.

At the end of the Cactus Rocks Trail, veer left (east, then south) onto the Vista Knoll Trail. Descend down the backbone of the ridge to some limestone balcones that afford views of Lake Travis. When Spanish explorers first saw the hills northwest of what is now Austin, they named the land "balcones" for the terraced and sometimes almost stairlike rock formations. The Great Plains and Gulf Coast geographic regions join at Balcones Canyonlands. Add to this the unusual limestone geology of the Edwards Plateau, and you've got the Hill Country, an area unique to central Texas. Limestone outcroppings sometimes cover the path, making walking difficult. Complete the loop and connect with the Ridgeline Trail, which leads left (northwest) to the Sunset Deck. The covered deck offers a view of Lake Travis while providing the opportunity to hear or see the black-crested titmouse, Carolina chickadee, and scrub jay, which are Hill Country specialties.

While backtracking to the intersection with the Vista Knoll Trail, watch for fox squirrels, named for their gray-and red-colored fur, which resembles the pelt of a gray fox. Those maple, oak, or pine trees you admire so much may have grown from the leftovers of a squirrel's unfinished meal. After reaching Vista Knoll, it is only a short distance to the intersection with the Cactus Rocks Trail and your return to the parking area. More than 525 plant species have been iden-tified within the refuge's boundaries. Included among these is the newly discovered Texabama croton, an 8- to 10-foot-tall shrub with white flowers in February and March.

Miles and Directions

0.0 Start at the Cactus Rocks trailhead, adjacent to the parking area, and head west on Cactus Rocks Trail toward the junc-tion with the Vista Knoll Trail.

0.6 Reach the T intersection with the Vista Knoll Trail. Take the left branch, heading south-southeast. Follow the trail, head-ing south, and stay left, following the loop clockwise and back to where it links with the Ridgeline Trail.

1.5 Ridgeline Trail joins Vista Knoll. Turn left (northwest) and follow the Ridgeline Trail to the Sunset Deck observation shelter.

2.3 Reach the Sunset Deck observation shelter at the end of the Ridgeline Trail. Backtrack to the intersection with the Vista Knoll Trail.

3.0 The Ridgeline Trail intersects the Vista Knoll Trail. Turn left onto Vista Knoll, heading north for a short distance to where the Cactus Rocks Trail intersects on the right (east). Turn right on Cactus Rocks and backtrack to the trailhead and parking area.

3.6 Arrive back at the trailhead at the Cactus Rocks parking area.

20 Bastrop State Park: Lost Pines and Scenic Overlook Trails

Combine portions of three trails into a 3-mile hike to see the best of Bastrop State Park. Start in the loblolly pines, towering 60 feet overhead. These are part of "Lost Pines," the westernmost stand in Texas. In the spring, mating calls from the Houston toad, an endangered species, can be heard. The park was designated a National Historic Landmark in 1997, based on work done in the 1930s by the Civilian Conservation Corps (CCC).

Distance: 3.1-mile loop
Approximate hiking time: 2 hours
Difficulty: Moderate (due to some steep inclines and narrow paths)
Trail surface: Forested dirt path, some rocky sections
Best season: September to June
Other trail users: Dog walkers
Canine compatibility: Leashed dogs permitted
Land status: State park; Texas Parks & Wildlife Department

Fees and permits: Day-use fee (or use the State Parks Pass); discount for Texas residents age 65 or older
Schedule: 8:00 a.m. to 10:00 p.m. daily. The Bastrop State Park lake, including the area surrounding it, and the section of the Lost Pines Trail that is east of Harmon Road are closed from February 22 to April 1 to protect the endangered Houston toad during the critical breeding period. Call Bastrop State Park

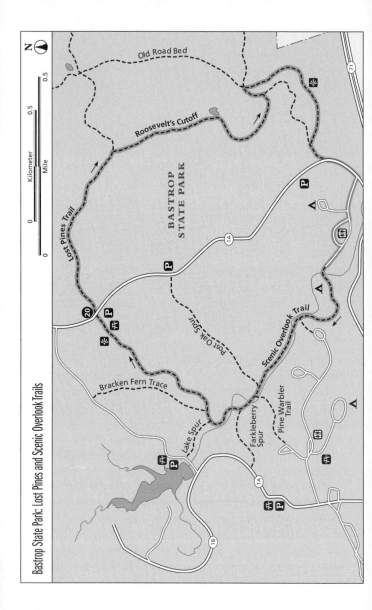

Bastrop State Park: Lost Pines and Scenic Overlook Trails

headquarters at (512) 321-
2101 for the latest information.
Be aware of ecosensitive areas.
Maps: Trail maps are available in
the park office. You can also find
maps on the Web site www.tpwd

.state.tx.us. NCGS topo: Bastrop,
7.5' quad
Trail contacts: Bastrop State
Park, P.O. Box 518/TX 21,
Bastrop 78602-0518; (512)
321-2101

Finding the trailhead: Bastrop State Park is located 30 miles
east of Austin. From Austin, take TX 71 into Bastrop. Turn left at TX
95 and follow signs to TX 21. The park entrance is on the left at the
intersection of TX 21 and 71. From the park entrance, follow Park
Road 1A almost 1.5 miles to the Overlook trailhead parking area.
DeLorme: Texas Atlas & Gazetteer: Page 70 H1. GPS: N30 06.451' /
W97 16.883'

The Hike

Start the Lost Pines Trail at the Lost Pines Overlook, adjacent to the parking area and across Park Road (PR) 1A. Be
sure to look at the brown sandstone shelter at the edge of
the parking area, constructed by the CCC in the 1930s and
still being used today. Then cross the road and go slightly
downhill and immediately into the Lost Pines.

These magnificent pines are isolated from the main
body of east Texas pines by nearly 100 miles—hence the
name Lost Pines. The 80-foot trees completely dominate
and virtually close off all views, while giving total shade.
All the trails shown on the Bastrop Park trail map (available
at the park office) are color coded: The Lost Pines Trail is
purple. Go through a gully and across a dry creek bed. This
short portion of the Lost Pines Trail loop soon comes to
the branch with Roosevelt's Cutoff, a short connector path
(orange on the map).

Head south and watch for the small Toad Pond on the left. Use caution around these ponds, as the Houston toad, an endangered species, breeds here. Make a sweeping right turn and come to an outcrop of sandstone near the connector T into the Lost Pines Trail. Take the right branch, heading south. Watch for large groups of bracken fern on both sides of the trail. A gate on the east side of PR 1A marks the end of the Lost Pines Trail. Cross the road and follow it into the Copperas Creek campground. Water, restrooms, and a shade shelter built by the CCC in the 1930s are available in the campground.

The park was designated a National Historic Landmark in 1997 due to the quality work done by the CCC. At the end of the campground, connect with the Scenic Overlook Trail (red on the map), proceeding north. Continue curving slightly left and go past the Piney Hill Spur on the left. Virginia creeper, a ground cover, can be seen off the trail. This is a good thing because Virginia creeper and poison ivy do not share the same ground. After the last intersecting branch, the Bracken Fern Trace, the Scenic Overlook Trail heads east back to the trailhead. On the fairly steep grade up to the trailhead, Eagle Scouts from Troop 1998 have built erosion fences and water bars.

Miles and Directions

- **0.0** Start at the Lost Pines Trail trailhead adjacent to the parking area.
- **0.3** The trail meets a Y. Turn right, heading south on the Roosevelt's Cutoff connector trail.
- **0.9** Roosevelt's Cutoff intersects and ends at the Lost Pines Trail at a T intersection. Take the right (south) branch of the Lost Pines Trail.

1.5 The Lost Pines Trail ends at Park Road 1A. Continue west and then north on Park Road 1A, passing over Copperas Creek and through the Copperas Creek Campground. There also are restrooms and water here.

1.8 The trail in the campground merges onto the Scenic Overlook Trail. Follow the Scenic Overlook Trail north.

1.9 Pass the branch to the Piney Hill Spur on the left (west). Continue to follow the Scenic Overlook Trail, passing a water fountain (not operational) built by the CCC in the 1930s.

2.2 Pass the branch to the Post Oak Spur on the right (east) and almost immediately pass the Pine Warbler Trail on the left (west). Continue on the Scenic Overlook Trail, heading north.

2.3 Pass the Farkleberry Spur on the left (west). Continue heading north for a short distance and then bear right (east).

2.6 Pass the Lake Spur on the left (north), then bear right, heading south and past the Bracken Fern Trace on the left (east). Head south for a short distance, and then bear left (east) and follow the Scenic Overlook Trail to the trailhead.

3.1 Arrive back at the trailhead and parking area.

About the Author

Keith Stelter is a columnist for the HCN newspaper group and has been hiking, writing, and taking photographs for forty years. Keith served as executive director of the Texas Outdoor Writers Association during 2006 and 2007. His other FalconGuides include *Best Hikes Near Austin and San Antonio* and Best Easy Day Hikes Guide to Houston and San Antonio. He is a member of the Outdoor Writers Association of America, Texas Master Naturalists, North American Nature Photographers Association, and American Trails Association. He resides in Tomball, Texas.